Mum's the Word

A guide to being a good mum in prison

Mary Stephenson
&
Bridget Lindley

Prisoners · Families · Communities
A Fresh Start Together

Mum's the Word
Mary Stephenson & Bridget Lindley

First published in the UK in 2014 by
Pact (Prison Advice and Care Trust)
Park Place
12 Lawn Lane
London
SW8 1UD

Produced by Bookworx
Editor Jo Godfrey Wood
Designer Peggy Sadler
Proofreader Anna Rader

A CIP record for this book is available from the British Library

ISBN: 978-0-9929773-0-6

10 9 8 7 6 5 4 3 2 1

 Printed through SS Media Limited

For further information see www.prisonadvice.org.uk

Contents

Foreword

Myself and other mums from HMP Eastwood Park and HMP Bronzefield have put this book together to help other mums who sadly end up in prison.

Being a prisoner and having a family and children "on the out" is so hard. Prison's easy – that's not a problem – but it's missing the kids that's hard. Us mums always talk about our kids together and when I first came to prison I didn't realise that there were so many ways that we can still keep in touch with our kids. That there are ways to let them know we still love them and think of them every single day. That's why we're writing this book: to help new mums who end up in prison. I really wish there had been a book like this to help us when I came to Eastwood Park.

Visits, letters and phone calls with our children are all that really keeps us going. We hope that this book will help you, with tips and ideas on how to keep the important bond between us mums and our kids.

We had a great time putting this book together, we made new friends, gave each other ideas and advice, and we all loved talking about our kids! We hope that you enjoy the book and that it gives you hope – that it helps you realise that you can still be a great mum even though you're in prison.

Mums in prison

"Go with the system"

"You are still their role model"

"Be proactive"

"Show your children constant love"

"Focus on what you already have"

"You can still play an active part in
your kids' lives"

(Some tips from mums serving life sentences)

Introduction

This book has been put together in collaboration with mothers at HMP Eastwood Park and HMP Bronzefield. They are the authorities on how you can still be a good mother while you are serving a prison sentence and separated from your children – they have experienced the challenges and have seen how they can be overcome. Some of these mothers were at the ends of their sentences and preparing to return home to their children, so they were able to demonstrate that there can be a happy ending.

The overwhelming advice from these mums was to "go with the system"; that at the end of the day you have no choice but to co-operate with the system (consisting of the prison, Probation and Children's Services) if you want to work towards release and being reunited with your children again as soon as possible. Time and again they stressed the importance of staying in touch with your children through letters, phone calls and, if possible, visits. Perhaps surprisingly, another piece of advice that the majority agreed on was that however difficult it might be, it is best to be honest with your children about where you are and why. They said that telling them you are in prison has to be done in a way that is suited to the child's age, but that it is really vital that they hear it first from you.

The importance of being realistic was another theme that frequently came up. They felt that a mother in prison had to be realistic with herself and, perhaps more importantly, with her children. However tempting it might be to tell your children that "Mummy will be home soon", if that isn't realistic then the children will be bitterly disappointed and lose the trust they place in you as their mother.

HM Inspectorate of Prisons sets down guidelines for prisons, known as "Expectations" and they refer to best practice in helping prisoners retain strong links with their families where this is permitted. We have included them in chapters 5, 7, 8, 9 and 10 because you may need to refer to an Expectation when putting in an application or going through the complaints procedure. Use the Expectations wisely: don't be tempted to throw them into an argument with a member of staff when you're angry.

The prison system is constantly changing, no more so than at the time of putting this book together, so we have tried to provide information that is relevant in the future as well. However, each prison is different and you will have to check that procedures such as accumulated visits or rules about being released on temporary licence (ROTL) are still the same as set out in this book. What doesn't change is the importance of the mother in a child's life, therefore much of this book is about how you can still play a central role in your child's life while you are in prison.

This book is not intended to be picked up, read from cover to cover and then put back on the shelf. We hope you will continue to dip into it and find it a constant source of encouragement and ideas, right from the start of your sentence through to release.

It contains many quotes from the women (and children) who helped us to put the book together. Each chapter deals with a different aspect of being a mother in prison, but there are central themes that run through all the chapters. In particular, we have added some suggested activities at the end of each chapter, which might be useful to help you develop a strong bond with your child – and they will also help you use your time well.

. . . .

✪ **Take heart.** You can be a good mother while you are in prison.

. . . .

This is our resident expert – the wise owl – and you will notice it liberally scattered throughout the book. Where you see it you are being urged to seek advice, information and/or support from an expert. These experts are there to help you and it is important to take full advantage of that help.

Be warned: when you talk to your expert, he or she may not necessarily say what you want to hear. But beware of shutting off from them. Instead, make an effort to listen properly. You can tell them what you were hoping their answer would be and ask why that isn't possible. Between the two of you, you may even find a way around your problem so that their answer fits better with your hopes.

"I wish Mummy could come home. I wish I could see more of her."

2 year old

"I wish I could be with Mummy."

20 month old

Your first night

Dealing with the shock

"I didn't even know where my kids were. In foster care? With the family? I just didn't know."

"You worry about your family and how it is affecting them."

"You worry about everything!"

When you first arrive in prison you are in such shock that it's hard to put your thoughts into sensible order. The information you're being given may be confusing. People may use words you don't understand and you're in no state to ask rational questions. This is all quite normal and it's important to give yourself time to adjust.

" It's the shock! You are in shock and can't take in anything they tell you."

Reassuring your family

Your family, particularly your children, will be very anxious to hear from you as they will want to know you are OK. Programmes about prisons on TV don't help – they tend to portray the dramatic side of prison life, so children can be very scared of what might happen to their mum when she's locked up with people who've been portrayed on TV as being scary. If you're able to reassure your family, that will help you to relax as well.

Your Reception Phone Call

"There's nothing you can do. Yeah, you can worry, but you've made that phone call, you know things are alright at home. You've just got to get on with it. You just have to make the best out of a bad situation."

" It's worse when you have kids; especially when you have sole responsibility for them."

ℹ **You are entitled to make a phone call (Reception Phone Call) on your first day.** If no one tells you about this, don't be afraid to ask – and keep asking until you get a satisfactory answer. If you feel frustrated by the responses you're getting, then ask to speak to the prison Chaplain. If, for some reason, you're not able to ring your family and reassure them yourself, the Chaplain will be able to ring them to tell them where you are and help set their minds at rest.

Your Reception Visit

Most prisons also allow a Reception Visit if you are a newly convicted prisoner. This should take place soon after you have been sentenced and you will be given a Visiting Order (known as a VO). You fill this in and it is then usually left at the Gate Lodge to await your visitor. For further visits the Visiting Order is sent to the visitor. If you're not given a Visiting Order or no one tells you that you can have a Reception Visit, don't be afraid to ask.

ASK AN EXPERT

Getting a visit

Ask the **Family Engagement Worker** to explain the procedure for having a Reception Visit.

Dealing with your emotions

Your emotions are quite likely to be all over the place – it's only natural. You've been through all the stress of your arrest and the court case, the publicity, the impact on your family and now your separation from them.

Your anger

"If you get stressed you're going to have attitude and be awful to the officers. And then things don't get done for you."

"You just have to bite your tongue and say to yourself; 'you know what, I can't do anything about it today. I'll just try again tomorrow.'"

For some people the overwhelming emotion is anger and frustration. It's all too easy to deal with this by seeking revenge on whoever you feel is responsible for your imprisonment, whether that's the judge, the police, a witness or the victim – or all of these. Another outlet for this rage can be kicking the system through refusing to do what is asked of you in prison, ranting and raving at the staff or adopting an attitude that puts up a barrier around you. These outlets might seem to provide comfort in the short term, but you won't be helping yourself in the long run.

"You can't go to bed thinking about it 'cos you won't sleep."

Your guilt

Give us women a reason to feel guilty and we'll grab it with open arms – especially when it comes to being a mum. But experiencing guilt never solves problems. Yes, you need to understand how your actions might have led you to be in prison, so that you avoid them in the future. But dwelling on where you went wrong is a waste of time. Instead, focus on how you can turn that around, to make sure it doesn't happen again.

Be honest about feeling guilty. What can you learn? Are these feelings affecting your relationship with your kids? Be honest, too, about what you already do well as a mum. Don't lose sight of these things; they are the building blocks for your future as a really great mum after you are released.

"Having no control to protect my kids was scary."

 ASK AN EXPERT

When you need support

When you need support, speak to someone – perhaps the **Chaplain** or the **Family Engagement Worker** – and tell them how you are feeling and what you are afraid of. Just getting these thoughts out of your head may help to put them into perspective.

When you've got those feelings out, don't fight any reassurances or suggestions the person might make. It's all too easy to cling on to your fears and tell yourself "they don't understand". Not only will these people have met many women feeling as desperate as you do now, but they will have seen mums who have gone on to maintain, and even strengthen, good relationships with their children in future years.

Your grief & fears

"I knew my parents wouldn't give me another chance and was frightened they wouldn't let me see my kids."

It is very natural to feel desperate loss when you arrive in prison. Some people describe separation from loved ones as a form of bereavement. The worst fears seem so real. Will your children be taken into care? Supposing something dreadful happens because you're not there to protect them. You're frightened that publicity in the papers will be seen by your family; how will it affect them?

Support for you

"To be a good mum you have to look after yourself, too."

"You have to ask for support and accept whatever help is available."

"A lot of people are afraid to go to the officers because if they're seen chatting to them they're frightened of what others might think, but at the end of the day, it's not about that. It's about how you can cope."

Your Family Engagement Worker

"I couldn't have coped without the Family Engagement Worker."

"She (the Family Engagement Worker) has been brilliant!"

"If it wasn't for the Family Engagement Worker I wouldn't be talking to my mum or my dad. She made that first phone call because I was scared of phoning my mum and her putting the phone down on me."

Hopefully by the time this book is in your hands, each female prison in England and Wales will have been assigned a Family Engagement Worker. When it comes to maintaining strong bonds with your family, and particularly with your children, the Family Engagement Worker is the person who is best placed to give you assistance.

Ask to speak to the Family Engagement Worker as soon as you can after you arrive in prison. When you make contact, be sure to ask what their name is, what days they come to the prison and how you can arrange to meet them in the future. However, if you are told that there is no Family Engagement Worker available to you, then ask to be referred to the member of staff who has particular responsibility for your links with your family.

On occasions, unfortunately, this request may be met with a blank stare or claims that there is no one available who has that responsibility. Prisons are large institutions and not all the staff know who has responsibility for what particular issues. However, all prisons have Chaplains and even if you do not have any religious beliefs, the Chaplaincy staff are there to help you in whatever way they can. Most staff will know who the Chaplain is and know how you can contact them.

"Try to get as much help as you can. If support is offered, inside and outside, take it."

"Rant to anyone who will listen!"

ASK AN EXPERT

Share your concerns

Speak to another **prisoner** you know you can trust and ask them any questions you have. If you're uneasy about sharing your concerns with just anybody (and women in prison often avoid getting too close to other prisoners until they know they can trust them), ask to speak to a **Listener**.

Listeners are prisoners who have been trained by the Samaritans to listen to fellow prisoners in times of need. You don't have to feel suicidal to speak to a Listener. They will keep what you tell them to themselves and regard it as confidential.

Other mothers

Forty per cent of women in prison are mothers. For 85 per cent of those, it is the first time that they have been separated from their children for any length of time. This means that you are surrounded by people who have been through these first terrifying days in prison and have shared the same worries and fears as you.

"Engage with services that are available to you."

Mentors & support groups

Some women's prisons have mentoring schemes or support groups, so ask if there are similar arrangements in your prison. It will help to hear that others have experienced the same fears as you. You might even find yourself being able to support someone else in the group and that can help make you feel stronger and less alone. By having a mentor or joining a support group you will find out about practical things you can do to help your children and keep the relationship with them strong.

✪ **Remember that in a support group**, just as you want others to treat your affairs with respect and confidentiality, so you will need to take care not to talk about other group members to anyone who is outside that group.

Get information & avoid feeling depressed

Depression is often caused by feeling that you have no control over your life – and prisons do make you feel as though you have lost control over what happens to you and your children. To avoid being overcome by that feeling and giving up and getting depressed, you need to get as much information as you can.

Once you have found your sources of support, don't be afraid to ask about such things as visits, phone credit, activities, jobs and courses available to you. Ask about Plain Paper Letters (PPL) and advocacy. A PPL means that the paper doesn't have any prison reference on it and can be used by a mum who doesn't want her children to know she is in prison. Prisoners receive one PPL letter per week for each child. Ask about your rights, too; this is very important at a time when you are feeling as though you have no rights at all. You do, and you can ask about advice from the Citizens Advice Bureau (CAB), solicitors and social services – some prisons have agency advisers coming in on a regular basis.

"Make sure you chase up your applications. Keep reminding them. And if you can't get an answer from an officer go higher; go to a Senior Officer (SO), a Custody Manager or even the Governor."

"Don't be afraid to ask for help."

....

Things you can do

....

The guilt-trip exercise

On a piece of paper draw up three columns (see next page). At the top of one column write "Negative". At the top of the second column write "Positive" and at the top of the third write "Action".

In the "Negative" column write down things you feel guilty about. In the "Positive" column, write down what you feel you do well as a mum. In the "Action" column write down what you will do to turn Negatives into Positives.

Your action plan

Once you have settled into being in prison, it's time to take stock of what you can do to make things better for you and your family. On a piece of paper make two columns (see next page). On the left-hand side write "My problem" and on the right-hand side put "How can I solve it?". Then fill in both columns. It may be easy to

"Put your troubles into a box and close it."

13

list your problems, but don't feel helpless if you can't, at present, come up with any solutions. Keep the list somewhere safe and as you gain more information, write down how you can solve problems. Just seeing how you can deal with situations will allow you to get problems out of your head and put them into a "box" to deal with it when you know how to.

Negative	Positive	Action
I'm separated from my kids.	I'm allowed contact with them.	Write a letter each week. Tell them I'll ring them at 7 pm each night to say good night.
I'm feeling really depressed.	Nothing!	Ask to speak to a Listener.
I'm missing my son's fourth birthday at the end of this month.	Can't think of anything positive about that.	Make a card for him with a picture of his favourite TV character on it. Find out about making a story CD for him.
My ex is dissing me to our daughter.	She told me she loved me on the phone.	Don't stoop to his level. Write to him and point out that this isn't helping your daughter.

My problem	How can I solve it?
Example: My mother won't let me speak to my kids on the phone.	Example: Ask the Chaplain or Family Engagement Worker to make the first phone call to explain everything for you.

Things to take from this chapter

✓ The feelings of shock, fear, anger and guilt on going to prison are all normal reactions.

✓ Don't lose sight of the positive things you can do for your children – just because you're in prison, it doesn't mean you can't still be a good mum.

✓ Use whatever help and support are available to you.

✓ Seek the information you need – don't be afraid to ask, and keep asking, until you get a satisfactory answer.

✓ As soon as you can, reassure your family, particularly your children, that you are OK.

Things I need to remember ...

CHAPTER TWO

Keeping in touch

That all-important contact

"My mum sends me letters sometimes, but we speak on the phone every day." 15 YEAR OLD

What will reassure your children most is hearing from you as often as possible. Phone calls, cards and letters – they will all help to maintain important bonds with your children, so even if you have run out of phone credit and don't like writing letters, try to find a way of keeping those links strong.

Sending letters

"Mummy sends me letters. I enjoy the pictures and jokes and they make me feel better." 6 YEAR OLD

"My mum sends me letters and cards." 3 YEAR OLD

Writing letters will help you feel better, and your children will love getting them. There is something special about seeing their name and no one else's on the envelope and it can be read over and over again. Lots of children like to keep letters from an absent parent in a special place; under their pillow or in a box. Then they can go back and remind themselves of their parent's love for them.

Try to think of something that will make your child smile or laugh. You may feel as though your world has come to an end, but you don't want your child feeling that way, too. See what you can add to your news that might help to lift their spirits.

"Mummy sends me letters and bracelets which she makes in her jewellery class." 5 YEAR OLD

"My mummy sends me cards. I like the pictures, drawings and colourings." 2 YEAR OLD

"I like the letters Mummy sends because they are pretty. She tells me what she has been doing." 5 YEAR OLD

If you are signing up for a course on Education, tell your children and joke about going back to school. If you have got a job in the prison, tell them about that and what it involves.

> *"Sending and receiving letters from my children is great and makes me feel close to them."*

If writing is not your thing, you could make a little cartoon of yourself to send your children – like a comic. It doesn't have to be long, but it should be positive. You could be really creative. Several prisons keep chickens – if this happens at your prison, then why not give the chickens names and make up little stories about them? Many prisons have drug dogs on the premises and it could help to prepare your children for their first visit if you tell them about the dogs, what their names are and what they look like.

Your teenage children may just think that this kind of thing is embarrassing. But even teenagers want to know that their mother is thinking about them, cares about them – even if they would never admit it – so it is still worth writing to them.

"I found writing a letter to the baby really helped."

✪ **Ask your children questions** about their lives; they may not reply to your letters, for whatever reason, but they will still be pleased that you are interested in what they are doing and take the trouble to write to them.

 ASK AN EXPERT

If your children aren't receiving your letters

You may suspect your children aren't receiving your letters because their carer is not passing them on. Or the carer may not be reading them to younger children. Keep a copy of each letter before sending it off. When you see your children, show them the copies, so that they can know that you did think of them and that you did write regularly. Is there a **relative** or **friend** who sees the children who could pass on your letters? In the meantime tell your **family solicitor** because if you are legally permitted contact with your children then regular contact should be taking place.

Making phone calls

"I like hearing her voice on the phone. She sends me cards and letters." 3 YEAR OLD

"I phoned my mum and my little boy came on the phone. As soon as I heard his voice I just broke down, you know what I mean? It hit me; reality set in."

✪ **It can be very emotional** to hear your children's voices on the phone, especially the first time you ring them. It is easier said than done, but try to be positive when you speak to them; your children will want to know you are OK.

If you do break down, it isn't the end of the world. It shows you love and miss your children. So don't ring off or avoid calling just because you're feeling emotional. Instead make sure your children understand that your tears are because you are happy to hear their voices; because you love them. Follow that explanation with reassurances that you are alright.

If you have only just arrived in prison and are too upset to speak to your family, contact the Family Engagement Worker and ask them to make that initial call to reassure them. If the Family Engagement Worker is not around, then you could ask one of the Chaplaincy staff if they could make the call.

"I phone and my mum says to him 'Mummy's on the phone' and he says, 'I'm playing!'"

"The other day my little boy said 'Can you call back later? I'm having my dinner. I'm not here right now.' That's what he told me on the phone. I just laughed. You can't take it to heart. I did [take it to heart] at first; it really upset me. Now I don't as long as he's happy."

As time goes by and your children settle in to the new routine, they may seem to be indifferent to your calls. This could be because they can't cope with their sense of grief and have shut down on that emotion. Losing a loved one to prison is often described as being like a bereavement, so remember that your children may well be feeling this deep sense of loss, which comes across (to you) as them not caring.

Young children, particularly, don't realise how difficult it can be for you to ring them, either because there is a long queue for the phone or because your phone credit has run out. They may say they are too busy to talk to you. This can be very hurtful, but try to put it into perspective. If they are feeling secure because you have done a great job of reassuring them, they may not even need to speak to you. You might have rung when they were in the middle of a very absorbing game or TV programme and because they don't understand the prison regime, they will think it's easy for you to ring back later.

If children know that you can't always get to a phone because it's being used by other people, or that there are times when you can't ring them, they will feel less upset if you are unable to ring.

Your children may have got into a routine and by phoning them after their bedtime you will not only possibly wake them up, but you will also get them excited and it could take a while to settle them after the call. If they have got to be up for school the next morning, then try to ring well before bedtime.

Your children's carer has their own life to live as well, so to maintain a good relationship with them, ask when it will normally be possible to ring and if they are out when you do ring, don't give them a hard time about it. Remember, the bottom line is to do what is best for your children. Falling out with their carer because they weren't in when you rang is not going to help.

"Just getting to see her when I visit is good."

12 year old

Your children's visits

"I like visiting my nan in prison, 'cos I love her." 3 YEAR OLD

"I like spending time with my auntie and seeing her when I visit her in prison." 14 YEAR OLD

"I enjoy spending time with my mum and seeing my brother." 6 YEAR OLD

"His behaviour changed [for the worse] at school. After he'd seen me, the social worker expected him to behave even worse at school, but he didn't, it calmed down after he'd seen me. His behaviour was fine after that. He needed to know I was OK, I think."

You may decide you don't want your children visiting you in prison, either because they don't know you are there or perhaps because you feel it will be too upsetting for them. But you need to be honest with yourself; is it really because you will find it too emotional? Is it because you don't know what to say to your children?

"The social worker wasn't going to bring my little boy up for a visit until the Family Engagement Worker got on the phone to them. They were worried about how he'd react when he had to leave the visiting room – things like that. In fact he was fine, but if it wasn't for the Family Engagement Worker, I wouldn't have had that visit."

 ASK AN EXPERT

If your children aren't allowed to visit

A social worker or a carer may have decided that it is better for your children not to visit you. If you disagree, ask for advice or get the **Family Engagement Worker** to ring the social worker and discuss what is best for your children. This will be a sensitive issue for you and you will understandably feel angry with the person who is apparently coming between you and your children. However, they will be more likely to agree to a visit if you discuss it calmly and rationally, listening to their views and putting your own across in a composed manner. Try a few practice runs with a friend or with the Family Engagement Worker before speaking to the social worker or carer.

"My little boy's school knew before he knew. That way the social worker could ask them to prepare him before the first visit."

"Face-to-face contact is no go 'cos I live in Cornwall and, like, it would be a six-hour journey for her; three hours up and three hours back. She's only four and it's too much for her."

There may be practical reasons why your children can't visit you. If this is the case then phone calls and letters are all the more important and need to be regular.

Preparing your children for a visit

Preparation is very important and can make all the difference between a successful visit and a disastrous one, so it is good if someone can explain to your children what to expect before the visit.

1 If children don't know about the drug dogs, they may panic when they are asked to stand still while the dog sniffs at them.

2 The searches can be another frightening experience for children, but if someone has explained it to them, perhaps likening it to searches they carry out at airports or museums, then the children will feel less threatened.

3 Children should be aware that they won't be able to take in their favourite teddy or toys because they would have to be taken away from them on arrival. This could be very distressing.

Your own preparation for a visit

Parents often say they don't know what to talk about on a visit – with children this can be particularly difficult. Here are some suggestions:

1 The journey to the prison may have been long and difficult for your children, so ask them how it was and be patient if they are grumpy.

2 Teenagers make a career out of being bad-tempered and hard to communicate with – so don't give up. Show your interest in them by asking after their friends; encourage them and be positive.

3 Prepare some games you can play at the table or topics for discussion with your younger children.

4 Agree with their carer to discuss any thorny issues and problems on the phone or by letter later – keep the visit as a warm and affectionate time.

5 If the prison allows it, encourage your children to bring in some school work to show you, so that you can perhaps help them with their homework.

6 After a visit or a phone call, make notes on what your children have told you about their life: the name of their best friend, the projects they are doing at school, their favourite subjects. Then next time you talk to them you can ask about those aspects of their world.

ℹ **In some prisons it can be arranged for you to have a video conference with your children,** so they can see that you are well. Ask the Family Engagement Worker if this is possible in your prison.

Dealing with the emotional side of a visit

"I just find it difficult to know what's best for the children. Like I really don't want them coming here, but then also they miss me and I miss them."

Visits are emotionally charged events and it is not just having to say goodbye to your children at the end which can leave you feeling stressed.

Your children may feel angry with you, particularly if they are teenagers. This is perfectly natural and arises out of their love for you. They want you to be in their life and at the moment they have to get along without you. Be patient with them and recognise that their anger is understandable – they will get over it if you give them time and love.

" Some kids don't understand why you can't stand up. My little girl, she'll want me to take her to the toilet and I don't know what to say to her."

Don't forget that even older children want to be loved by their mum. They may not admit to it. They may even snarl at you for giving them a hug, saying you are being embarrassing. But secretly they would rather you showed your love for them than not; we all need to be loved, particularly by our mums.

⊗ **On occasions you may be expecting a visit from your children and they don't turn up.** This can be for any number of reasons: traffic hold-ups, missing a train, a lift not arriving. This kind of disappointment is awful for you, but remember that it's awful for your children, too. If it is because their father or carer has decided not to bring them for some reason, then your anger could lead you to blame them when you are talking to your children. Try to avoid this as it will only make your children feel torn between two people they love.

What if you can't have visits?

There may be occasions when your children can't visit you. But don't worry, there are plenty of other things you can do that will be almost as good.

Try recording stories

Most prisons have a facility whereby you can record stories for your children which are then sent to them. Even if you don't read well, there is usually a way of editing mistakes during the recording to make it sound as if you can!

Don't assume that because your children are older there is no point in recording anything for them. They will still want to hear your voice and you can record letters to them.

ⓘ **Some prisons do the "You and Your Mum" project,** which is aimed at children aged 8 to 18 and run by "Storybook Mums" – ask if they run such projects for mums and children at the prison.

Children absolutely love receiving these CDs and often say they listen to them when they are missing their mum. Babies get to know their mum's voice and if there is a big gap between visits, it means they recognise their mum's voice and know the person they are visiting is someone special who cares for them.

Children who are learning to read can benefit if they have a copy of the written story to look at as well. It helps them to learn to read; while they listen to you telling the story, they can follow the words on the page.

Making memory boxes

Some mothers aren't allowed to have contact with their children, in which case they need to prepare for the future, either for when contact is allowed or for when their children are old enough to ask about their mum. In this situation a mum can start putting together a memory box for the children, so that one day they will know that their mother loved them.

Memory boxes can contain anything that shows your children they have been in their mum's thoughts, including:

- Letters written regularly to your children.
- A diary or journal written for the children telling them about you (their mum), your own childhood and your family.
- Pictures painted specially for your children.
- Poems.
- Birthday cards.
- Soft toys made for your children in prison.

Collecting photos

When people are asked what they would save first if their house was on fire, they often say they would save their family photos. Photos are so important to us and never more so than when we are separated from those we love. So ask for photos of your children to be sent in to prison – not just at the start of your sentence, but throughout it, so you can see your children developing.

On family days there is often the opportunity to have your photo taken with your children for them to take home afterwards. Don't worry about not looking good in these photos, your children will love to have a photo of you, even if you don't think it's a particularly flattering one. You will be allowed to have a photo of your family taken at the family day, which you can keep once it has been cleared by security.

> "I love the CD my nan recorded for me. We played it in the car on the way to prison today."
>
> 3 year old

Celebrating birthdays & holidays

"Mummy sends me cards and pictures." 3 YEAR OLD

"I miss not seeing my daughter on her first Christmas and missing my younger son's first school Christmas concert."

"I miss not being able to watch them open presents and see their faces light up."

Birthdays and holidays, such as Christmas, are so special for children – it makes it even harder when you know you can't spend them with them. There are usually family days around Christmas time in prison, so make sure you put your name down for any that might be happening. Don't leave it too long because these events get booked up.

"It's hard at first, but it gets easier."

You can buy cards and small gift items from the prison canteen, but it is much nicer for children if they receive something that has been made especially for them by their mum, who knows the kind of things they like. In addition, you keeping busy is the best way of making your time go faster and if you fill it with making things for your children you will be helping them get through this tricky time as well.

 ASK AN EXPERT

Try craft projects

You can send off for craft kits or get a book out of the **library** which shows how to make soft toys or presents. Ask in the **Education** department for any opportunities to do craft work and for any help or advice that they may be able to give you.

Some parents say it's easier to treat special days as just another day, but your children will need to know that you have remembered them on those special days. This doesn't just mean at Christmas or on birthdays, but also if they are playing a part in the school concert or participating in sports day. Try to send a card before any special day and then ring your children afterwards to find out how the event has gone.

 **ASK AN EXPERT**

Find out what projects are available

Ask the **Family Engagement Worker** if the following are available in your prison.

- The Prison Fellowship is a charity which runs a project called "Angel Tree", where they will buy, wrap and deliver a present at Christmas to prisoners' children. Sometimes they also provide presents for prisoners to give their children on other special days or at a prison family day.

- At Christmas, the National Society for the Prevention of Cruelty to Children (NSPCC) runs a project called "Send a Letter from Santa". You fill in a form with the name and address of the children you want a special letter from Santa sent to. The forms are usually available from the Chaplaincy. Normally they request a donation, but if you can't afford that and explain that you are in prison, they will send the letter anyway.

Things you can do

✏ Create a comic strip

If you don't feel happy about writing letters, why not make a comic strip that can tell your children about an aspect of your daily life? It's perfectly OK to use stick people and just add speech or thought bubbles.

Most newspaper comic strips are only three pictures long, so you don't need to produce a whole page to make a story. Get hold of some newspapers and look at their comic strips. Then try out some ideas yourself. It is often easier to do this with someone else, so why not ask a friend who might be interested in doing the same for their children?

One comic strip a week will be enough to show your children you are thinking of them and give them an idea of what you are up to. You can even create them as a series, with each comic strip ending on a cliff-hanger, so that the children are keen to receive the next one to find out what happens next.

What to do on visits

What games can you play and what activities can you do with your children without having to move from your seat on a visit? Here are some ideas:

- I-Spy.
- Hangman – this one helps your children learn spellings, too.
- Noughts and crosses.
- Telling "knock, knock" jokes.

See if you can think of other games you can play or you could even make one up that is special for you and your children. One man devised games he could play over the phone with his 5-year-old son. They even played hide and seek with the boy really hiding and calling out, "Where do you think I am now, Daddy?" When his dad made a guess, the little boy would tell him whether he was getting warmer or not. Have a go at thinking what games you can play on the phone, but make them short so that you don't run out of credit.

Watch their favourite TV programmes

If your children have favourite TV programmes, then make an effort to watch them as well, so you can discuss them with them when they visit you or when you chat on the phone.

Make a memory box

You don't have to be denied contact with your children to justify making them memory boxes. Plan a memory box to make while you are in prison, showing your kids how much you have been thinking about them (see pages 23 and 66).

Things to take from this chapter

✓ It is really important to keep up regular contact with your children while you are in prison.

✓ If you think your children aren't receiving your letters, make copies before sending them off. Then ask a trusted friend or family member to pass on the letters to them.

✓ Letters don't have to be long, but if you don't feel happy writing them, try drawing comic strips.

✓ Try not to ring your children at awkward times for the carer, such as after bedtime.

✓ Phone calls can be emotional, especially the first one you make. Ask the Family Engagement Worker to make the call for you so your children are reassured that you are OK.

✓ If possible ask your children's carer or school to prepare them for the visit, so that they are ready for things like searches and drug dogs.

✓ Younger children really appreciate having a recording of their mum reading them a bedtime story; it helps them feel close to you.

✓ Visits can be difficult if you don't know what to say – prepare games to play with your children while you are all seated at the table or think up some good topics for discussion.

✓ There are projects that provide presents at Christmas for children of prisoners – ask your Family Engagement Worker about these.

✓ If your children run to their carer when they are unhappy on a visit, it doesn't mean they don't love you. It shows they feel comfortable with their carer and that's a good thing.

✓ Your children might say they are too busy to take your call; it's probably because they are feeling secure and think you can ring them back when they've finished what they are doing. Don't take this rebuff personally.

"Mum's in a castle!"

Telling children that their mum is in prison needs to be handled very sensitively. There are so many factors to consider, depending on the children and individual circumstances. However, the trust of your children is so important that to be honest with them really is the best thing you can do. It's how you tell them that matters.

Thinking about age-appropriateness

"It's age-dependent, how you prepare your child."

A baby or toddler is unlikely to understand the concept of prison, but don't underestimate even pre-school children's ability to work out that something is wrong. One little boy was two when his dad went to prison, so his mother and older sisters agreed that they would tell him that Daddy was working away. When they visited the prison, it was explained that Daddy was working there. The boy was five when his dad returned home and for years the family congratulated themselves on being able to keep the truth from him. However, several years later one of his sisters, out of curiosity, asked him where his dad had been for those years and he replied in a very matter-of-fact voice:"in prison".

"They came and got us at 8 o'clock in the morning. I didn't have a chance to grab anything: no clothes, nothing."

✪ **Even very small children can sense that something is wrong** when they enter a room and the grown-ups stop talking, or their granny and older siblings are moody or upset. Not knowing why they are behaving like this can be more frightening than being told the truth.

When you are in prison, there is every chance that your children will have to move and be cared for by someone else who has a different routine. All this is going to convince even a toddler that something major has happened.

Your children may have been present when you were arrested and have suffered the trauma of seeing their mum taken away by the police – a not uncommon occurrence. Even very young children are going to find it hard to accept the story that their mum was going off to work. Then there is the publicity. Local journalists love to make a story that's going to sell their newspapers and the bigger the story the better. Even if a child is too small to read, there are older children who can and who may not be as discreet as you would like them to be.

⭐ **Everyone loves to gossip** and children pick up on this, too. If they have started going to school they may be bullied because of the stories, exaggerated probably, going round about their mum (see also page 57).

If you haven't told your children that you are in prison, then you may not want them visiting because it's so hard to conceal the fact that you are in prison. They will see prison notices and officers, who may mention prison in conversation within their earshot. Children will be puzzled by the need for a dog sniffing them and possibly being searched. They won't understand why, if their mum is just there to work, she isn't allowed to get up from her seat and play with them in the play area.

But if you don't want them to visit, they may feel it's because you don't want to see them.

"My kids say to me 'Why can't I come home?' and I'm like, 'cos Mummy and Daddy weren't very well'. Now my daughter, she's five now, she sits on my lap and says, 'Mummy, you look better now, can you come home?'"

"My daughter thinks I'm a nurse."

"I tell her, 'Mummy's house isn't big enough, but as soon as I get a bigger place you can come and stay'."

Then again, if you do have your children to visit, what do you tell them about where you are and why you are there? So what are the points for and against telling them the truth? (See chart on page 30.)

You may be able to add to this debate with reasons both for and against. Think everything through, talk things over with other mothers in the prison and the Family Engagement Worker.

The important thing is that you discuss everything with your children's carer and the family because you don't want them

"My mum and dad have had to keep the newspapers away from my son 'cos he's a good reader."

"It's my thing to tell my children where I am."

telling your children one thing while you tell them another. It may be that they have insisted the children are not told and so the matter has already been taken out of your hands.

Whether to tell your children or not

For	Against
"It's about teaching your kids honesty as well. It's like I want my kids to come to me if they've got any problems. By me being honest with them now I'm thinking that they can be honest with me in the future."	"It could upset them and confuse them." It is more confusing, though, if children know something is wrong, but no one will talk to them about it.
"It's teaching them boundaries isn't it? When you're a child you get the naughty step. When you're older you come to a place like this."	"You don't want them thinking bad of you." If you tell them what the truth is, you can reassure them. If you don't, they will eventually find out and lose their trust in you.
"You need to let them know, so they don't resent you when they're older."	"Stereotyping, images from TV and things." If you tell them the truth, then they can talk with you about their fears, based on the stereotyping, and you can reassure them.
Even if your children can't read, the publicity about your case will get around and they may learn a distorted version of the truth from a child at school.	What might seem like a short sentence in prison to you will seem like a lifetime to small children.
	You can devise something to help them with this, like an advent calendar, with milestones for each month that has gone by and pictures to celebrate.
You won't have to live a lie when your children visit you.	
On family days and special visits you will be able to relax more and apply for longer visits without fear of your children finding out.	
Your children will be able to talk more freely about their feelings to you or their carer.	

 **ASK AN EXPERT**

If you want your children to know the truth

If you retain parental responsibility and want your child to know the truth about where you are, speak to the **Family Engagement Worker** to discuss the best course of action.

✪ **Reassure your children** that you're OK; let them know where you are. Let them know that one day you will be back with them. Whatever ages your children are, even if they are angry with you and refuse to talk to you, they will want to know that you are OK.

Who else do you tell?

One mother of a 13-year-old boy, when she knew her story was about to become common knowledge, was brave enough to go and see the mother of her son's best friend. She realised that it might mean the other mother would stop the boy from associating with her son. In fact the other mother was sympathetic and talked it through with her son, encouraging him to support his friend. This meant that the mother going to prison knew her son could turn to his best friend for help.

✪ **You may have more than one child and each will be different** according to their age, their sensitivity and their wellbeing, so although you will not want to give kids totally different explanations for your absence, you may need to take different approaches in how you tell them.

If yours is an only child and they know you are in prison, you will be able to encourage them to meet other children on a family day, so they don't feel they are the only child with a mum in prison. As well as the school being told, consider writing to others who may be able to support your child, such as their local doctor.

Things that you can do

☞ Make a countdown calendar

Design a calendar, similar to an advent calendar, counting down the days, weeks or months (depending on the length of your sentence) with a treat at each milestone such as a door to open on to a funny picture, or a card you have made to send to them to celebrate passing that milestone.

☞ Make a list of people

Make a list of the important people in your children's lives and anyone who may be able to support them. Beside each name write down the points you would like to make to that person, so that they can be helped in adapting their care to suit your children.

☞ Think up questions and answers

Your children will have lots of questions for you and although you can't be expected to anticipate all of them, think of the obvious ones and devise answers that are honest but appropriate for each child.

Things to take from this chapter

✓ Honesty with your children is very important. It's how you tell them the truth that matters.

✓ You probably know your children best, but think first before you tell them. Speak to other mothers in prison and the Family Engagement Worker. Agree with the whole family and the carers what you will tell them, so that the children don't receive conflicting stories.

✓ Children pick up an atmosphere and know things are wrong even when they are very little – don't assume that because they are young they will think that everything is OK.

✓ Let the school, your local doctor and other people who can support your children know.

✓ Whatever you tell your children, reassure them that you are OK. Don't forget to reassure older children too – they do care, honestly!

✓ There is bound to be some publicity and gossip in your local area, so if you think your children are at all likely to hear it, talk or write to them as soon as possible, so that they are prepared.

✓ Think carefully before saying you don't want your children to visit you; children very easily feel rejected and they might think it's because you don't want to see them.

Things I need to remember ...

Who needs money?

Unfortunately we all do. While you are in prison you will get the chance to earn some pocket money to buy tobacco, toiletries, postage and phone credit. However this money doesn't go far. So how are you going to help your struggling family financially? How are you going to pay for Christmas and birthday presents for your children? What are you going to live on when you are released?

In prison you have two options: Work or Education. So what are the points in favour of each? See if you can think of any other benefits of either Work or Education.

Work versus Education in prison

Working in prison	Education in prison
It may not pay much, but at least you are keeping yourself busy and getting a bit more, if you're lucky, than you do on Education.	Education may not pay much, but if you get some qualifications, then you may be able to earn more when you are released.
Some prison jobs are paid quite well.	You have a range of courses to choose from.
Working in prison gives you more freedom.	You can gain skills and knowledge.
You gain confidence for when you are released.	Education challenges you, so you learn what you are capable of as a person.
You can get good work experience.	Education keeps you busy.
You'll learn work discipline, such as following rules and getting to work on time.	Education gives you more freedom in prison.
You meet different people at work in prison.	Education gets you off the wing.
You can gain office skills, such as on computers.	Education's irregular – more flexible than work.
You gain trust from authority figures.	You gain confidence.
You acquire a sense of self-worth.	Education helps you get a job after release.
Work in prison can make you feel wanted.	You meet new people.

Make your own list here about Work versus Education

It is very frustrating when you know your family, who may be supporting your children, are struggling financially. It is easy to feel guilty and helpless. Although you probably can't help them financially while you are in prison, there are other ways of assisting them with their finances.

Getting advice

It is possible that it is easier for you to get advice about benefits and debt management while you are in prison than it is for your family outside. For example, your children's grandparents may have difficulty travelling to the advice centre, your sister might have her hands full looking after her own children plus yours. Your young children wouldn't know how to go about getting advice and wouldn't be familiar with the terms used. However in prison

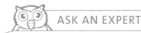 ASK AN EXPERT

Find out about the Assisted Prison Visits Scheme

If your family are on benefits and can't afford to bring your children to visit you, they may qualify for help with the costs. Ask your **Family Engagement Worker** to tell you about the Assisted Prison Visits Scheme.

at least part-time representation from various advice agencies is provided. Take advantage of what's on offer and get as much information on benefits and financial support to help your family as you can.

Transfer to open prison

As your release date draws closer, you may be transferred to a prison where you will have the chance, after a while, to get a job outside the prison. This will enable you to earn more money and as you are not paying board and lodging, it is a good opportunity to save in preparation for your release.

Even if you don't go to an open prison, you should be using the available information to get as much advice as possible about support after your release. The benefit system has gone through a lot of changes, so you may need to update your knowledge. If you don't understand terms in use, don't be afraid to ask.

Sorting out debts

You may have had debts when you came into prison. Even if you didn't, they may well be mounting up for you now as bills come in but you aren't at home to pay them. Don't stick your head in the sand and hope they'll go away. They won't. However, you will be surprised how understanding creditors can be if you contact them quickly and assure them you intend to get advice on a debt-management plan to help pay them off gradually. People who are owed money feel far more tolerant of debtors who are open

 ASK AN EXPERT

Managing your debts

Once you have contacted whoever you owe money to, then you need to find out about getting advice from the **Citizens Advice Bureau** or an honest debt-management organisation that can help you put a plan into place.

with them and want to do all they can to pay them back. However, tolerance will wear thin if you don't carry out your plan. It is no good making promises but not carrying them through or just coming up with more excuses. That way you will lose good will and even if you are telling the truth, they won't believe you.

Buying presents

When we've got money it's very tempting to buy expensive presents for children and think that this is enough to show them (and everyone else) how much we love them. At first children are thrilled: "Look what my mum bought me!" is met by "oohs" and "aahs" from friends. The suggestion is "they must love you very much" and children feel "I must be worth loving".

But if those expensive presents are not backed up by the parent listening to their children, showing their interest in what they are doing or making the time to spend with them, the children start to see this as proof that maybe they aren't worth spending time with, that they don't have anything to say worth listening to. No matter how many expensive presents the children may receive, if they don't get love and attention when the novelty of a new present wears off, what will they have then?

✪ **It is important to keep yourself busy in prison,** and what better way to do that than by making something for your child? The art department in Education can probably help. Or you can get a book out of the library which shows you how to make toys. If you have a bit of money, some prisons allow you to buy kits for making soft toys.

Keeping up your insurance

As if you didn't have enough on your plate, if you have any insurance on your car or your home, it may be affected by your being sent to prison.

ℹ **Unlock is a charity** which offers advice on criminal convictions. They produce a simple guide to insurance. Their contact details are at the back of this book (see page 96).

Writing a will

You don't have to be old, ill or in danger to write a will. Many people write one as soon as they become a parent because they want to make sure their children inherit from them in the unlikely event that they die unexpectedly. Even if it is just to ensure that

ASK AN EXPERT

Ask for help in making your will

You can ask someone to get a simple will form from WHSmiths and send it to you. Then ask someone (e.g. your **family solicitor** or a **Citizens Advice Bureau worker**) for help and advice on filling it in.

your child gets the special brooch which your grandmother left you, it's worth making a will. Wills can always be altered as your circumstances change, so if you haven't already made one, think about doing so now.

Things you can do

Plan ahead

- Talk through any financial concerns you have with your family and find out what advice you can get through agencies who come into the prison.
- Plan for your children's birthday or Christmas presents ahead of time. When your children are old enough, be open with them about your lack of money and explain that although their presents at Christmas or birthdays may be smaller than they used to be, your love for them is just as big as ever. You will be surprised how understanding even little children can be.
- See what you can make for your children's presents – ask in Education, look in the prison library for craft books, look at catalogues for craft kits.
- Write a list of the things you would want your children to have if anything happened to you. These things don't have to be valuable – even small items of sentimental value should go into a will.
- Find out what courses are available in Education, to improve your earning prospects when you leave prison.
- Find out what jobs are available in the prison so that you can earn some extra money now.

Useful tips

○ If you don't want to be transferred to another prison, get yourself a job in the prison that puts you on hold, so that you don't get moved even further away from your family (for example, apply to become a Listener).

○ Make sure your positive behaviour at work, on the wing or in Education is recorded on your prison records, so that you can start working towards enhanced status and qualify for more visits.

Things to take from this chapter

✓ If your family are receiving benefits they may qualify for financial assistance towards the cost of visiting you – ask about the Assisted Prison Visits Scheme.

✓ It is possible to save money while you are in prison – find out what jobs are available and what wages are paid. Weigh this up against the Education courses available and how beneficial those qualifications will be when you are released.

✓ Debt advice is available through agencies that visit the prison.

✓ Even though you are not likely to die soon, it is still worth writing a will to ensure that your children get what you want them to eventually.

✓ If you are likely to be transferred to an open prison, find out what opportunities there are to gain work placements in the community there.

✓ Don't get yourself deeper into debt in order to buy your children expensive presents. Explain to them that money is a little tight at the moment and find out about making presents for your kids instead.

✓ Contact the organisations and people to whom you owe money and reassure them that you will be setting up a plan for repayment of those debts over time – then do just that.

✓ Check that you are still covered under your home and car insurance policy.

CHAPTER FIVE

Mother & baby units

Currently there are five prisons which have Mother and Baby Units:

- Bronzefield – Ashford, Surrey.
- Eastwood Park – near Wotton-Under-Edge, Gloucestershire.
- Styal – Wilmslow, Cheshire.
- New Hall – near Flockton, Wakefield, West Yorkshire.
- Peterborough – Peterborough, Cambridgeshire.

There is also a Mother and Baby Unit for mums under 18 at the Rainsbrook Secure Training Centre, near Rugby, Warwickshire.

All Mother and Baby Units have their own routines and conditions, so this information is for guidance only and you will have to be prepared to adapt to the particular set-up of the Mother and Baby Unit you apply for.

Who can apply?

A mother with a child under 18 months of age can apply to have her child in prison with her on a Mother and Baby Unit. Their application is considered by the Admissions Board, who look at and discuss what is best for the child in the short and long term. They are reluctant to accept women whose sentences are longer than the point at which their child reaches 18 months of age.

If you are on drugs, you have to come off them and be on Methadone before you will be considered for a place in a Mother and Baby Unit.

CASE STUDY

One woman was refused a place for herself and her new baby as social services said he was going to be adopted. After he was born he was removed from the hospital and put into foster care. The mother fought the decision all the way to the High Court and won, gaining permission to have her baby on the Mother and Baby Unit with her.

Apply to go on the Mother & Baby Unit

If you are pregnant when you go to prison you should fill out an application form to apply to go on the Unit after the birth. You should check with the **Family Engagement Worker** when this application can go in.

Once you have applied to go on to the Mother and Baby Unit, you will not be moved from the prison while your application is still being considered.

When does the child have to leave?

The age at which the child has to leave varies with each prison, but it is seldom younger than 18 months unless the mother has very little time left to serve, in which case it may be considered best for the child to remain with the mother until she is released.

As the child gets nearer to the age when they must leave, preparation for that separation from their mother starts. This usually means that the child spends time with the outside carer and the family are allowed to come into the prison more often. Following the separation, the mother is usually allowed extra all-day visits with her child.

Staffing of the Units

All Mother and Baby Units employ nursery staff, who look after the children while the mother is working or on Education during the day. During this time the nursery staff often take the babies out of the prison to get them used to being outside. Some units keep an information file to record what activities the nursery staff have carried out with the babies.

There are regular visits from specialists, who meet with the mother and check on the health and development of both herself and her baby. Health visitors also come in to the Mother and Baby Unit on a regular basis.

Records are kept of the baby's progress and for those mothers who have low literacy levels or who don't speak English these records may be kept in a visual format.

HM Inspectorate's Expectations for Mother and Baby Units (extract)

- Provision is made for co-parents to be involved in antenatal care and preparation with their pregnant partners at the prison.
- There is a clear, effective and fair admissions policy. Women have access to easily understood information about the prison, its statement of purpose and function and written procedures and documentation for application, admission and separation.
- Admission, review and separation policies and childcare and protection arrangements are agreed with the Local Safeguarding Children Board.
- Children have opportunities to experience community activities and are prepared to leave the prison in accordance with their development needs and best interests.
- Visiting arrangements are as natural as possible for co-parents visiting their children, for grandparents and for the child's siblings.
- Pregnant prisoners and prisoners with children are fully supported throughout their time at the prison by appropriately trained custody staff.
- Care planning starts from the earliest knowledge of pregnancy or following the mother's admission to custody.
- Initial planning meetings and review meetings are attended by the mother.
- Planning and review meetings focus on the child's needs and how the mother can best be helped and supported to meet them. The mother's sentence plan complements and supports the child's care plan.
- Child development is monitored and arrangements are in place to access relevant services and specialists if issues arise.
- Mothers and staff have the knowledge and training to deal with child emergencies, including resuscitation and choking.
- Mothers are able to exercise parental responsibility through informed choices.
- Mothers from minority ethnic backgrounds and with differing childcare traditions are supported and the facilities and decor reflect a multiracial and multicultural community.
- Where a child is separated from its mother before the mother's discharge date, the mother is fully supported both emotionally and practically in making the arrangements for separation. Counselling services are available for those who have experienced loss or bereavement.
- All staff working with children have undergone specific recognised training including child protection issues and infant resuscitation and have been subject to enhanced CRB checks.

"During the day when they've got the nursery staff there to look after them, you have to make the best of that and do Education to get qualifications, or get work to try and save some money. You're not going to get free childcare when you're out."

Visits

"Sometimes now she'll say to me, 'Can we go to your other work Mummy, 'cos I want you to come and play with me'. She's remembered how we could play together on visits in the Mother and Baby Unit."

Visits are held on the Unit and not in the Visit Hall like the rest of the prison. This enables the extended family to meet with the baby and mother in a much more suitable environment. Some units organise special Family Days on the Unit for visitors, mothers and babies.

ⓘ **The child is also allowed to go on special home leave** with the family, but the mother has to request it and the carer has to be approved before the Governor will sign consent.

"Do everything you can before you go onto the Mother and Baby Unit; get your enhanced status and make sure you've got good behaviour [recorded]."

Once you have reached enhanced status this will allow you to have more visits and also apply for Release on Temporary Licence (ROTL), which allows you and your baby to have much more time with the family outside.

Supporting each other

Generally mothers find it helps being with others going through the same experience with their babies. However, the atmosphere can be tense through jealousy over who gets ROTL, with mothers falling out because their babies squabble or pinch each other's toys.

"It can be difficult, you know, getting on together on the Unit. There's all sorts of arguments about the kids, what they've got, what they haven't got. You just have to adapt and not let it get to you. You've got your kid with you; that's what matters."

Things to take from this chapter

✓ Currently there are only five Mother and Baby Units – Bronzefield, Eastwood Park, Styal, New Hall and Peterborough. Also there is one at Rainsbrook Secure Training Centre for mothers aged under 18.

✓ If you are turned down for the Unit, you may be able to obtain legal advice and lodge an appeal.

✓ Mother and Baby Units have trained nursery staff to look after the babies during the day. Sometimes they take them out of the prison to get them used to the outside world.

✓ A baby can only stay on a Mother and Baby Unit up to the age of 18 months; in some units they have to leave when they are younger than that.

✓ A mother with a child under 18 months of age can apply to have her child with her in the Mother and Baby Unit, but the screening process is very strict.

✓ Mothers are supportive of each other, but jealousies can also set up tension – you just have to tolerate these and make the best of it.

Things I need to remember ...

CHAPTER SIX

Your emotional roller coaster

Let's think about you

Being a mother is like being on an emotional roller coaster; getting into trouble sets the roller coaster going faster. And going to prison? Wow! That particular roller coaster tosses you here, there and everywhere. No wonder you feel like screaming.

We women embrace guilt. We may be tempted to deny everything, to blame everyone else, but deep down we feel gutted that somehow we are the cause of all the trauma that has hit our family. These feelings drag us down and make us feel worthless. When you feel like that it's so hard to convince your family that you are OK. Yet your children need your reassurance that you will be alright. So it's time to start pampering yourself and building up your own self-esteem, so you can support your family and, in turn, lift their spirits.

Mirror, mirror

Since coming into prison you probably haven't bothered much about the way you look – what's the point? The point is that when you look in the mirror each day you need to like what you see. That positive feeling can start with your appearance and work its way in to your feelings of self-esteem. This is also part of reassuring your children; when they come to visit, you want them to see you looking well.

ℹ️ **Most women's prisons have a Hair and Beauty Department on Education,** where you can get your hair cut or be given makeovers by students. You may even become interested in learning hairdressing or beauty therapy yourself, so that while you learn you can understand how to make the best of yourself. Get advice from other students and even try out a new hairstyle or style of make-up.

Education, education

Did you enjoy learning at school? If you spent most of your school days either bunking off with your friends or day-dreaming at the back of the class, then now is the time to make up for your misspent youth. Take a good look at yourself – this time not in the mirror, but at your strengths and interests. Many successful people left school having passed few, or no, exams, but instead found their real path as adults and gained qualifications at college.

✪ **Even if you have already got some qualifications,** now is an ideal time to refresh those skills or build on them.

Going to college costs money and as a mother you are going to have to fit any course around childcare. Not in prison you don't! This is the perfect opportunity to enrol for education and prove wrong all those people who said you were useless when you were busy bunking off school. Probably your biggest doubter was yourself; now's the time to prove to yourself that you do have a brain.

See what courses are on offer. Choose one you are interested in and ask other women who have done it whether it is any good or not. Ask what the teacher is like – a good teacher can make virtually any subject interesting.

Don't be afraid to tell your kids you have gone back to school. It will give you something to talk about with them. If they are older and studying the same subject, you might even be able to ask their advice; kids love it when their parents admit that their children are smarter than they are.

Talking to someone you trust

You may be feeling so disheartened that all this talk of pampering and education might seem a bit pie in the sky. If that's the case then the most important step is to tell someone you can trust how you are feeling. Remember the Family Engagement Worker and the Chaplaincy team are there to support you and help you deal with difficult emotional times.

ⓘ **Listeners are prisoners** trained by the Samaritans to help other prisoners. You can request a Listener at any time, night or day, and an officer will bring one to you. What you tell the Listener will be treated with absolute confidentiality. So do please talk to them. If you can't accept that you are worth this kind of attention, remember that your children are. It may seem as though life has ended for you, but it hasn't. When you reach rock bottom, the only way is back up again.

Others are there to help you too: the Chaplaincy team, the Family Engagement Worker and the Healthcare staff. Don't be afraid to tell an officer how you are feeling. That will alert them to your vulnerability and someone will check regularly to see you are alright. No one will laugh at you. These feelings are too serious to make jokes about. You will be taken seriously and supported until you feel less unhappy. Once you are feeling stronger you can start helping your family.

"You want to wrap them in cotton wool. You don't want them ever to experience this."

Your children's emotions

Swooping up and down with you in that roller coaster car is your family. They too are being thrown all over the place emotionally. As a mother you naturally want to protect your kids from fear and harm. And it doesn't help that you know they are up and down because of something you have been accused of or something that has happened to you.

You are human and as humans we all make mistakes. Some of them are terrible mistakes. How you deal with those mistakes is what really matters now.

✪ **Remember your children may have a strong protective feeling for their carer,** particularly if it is their father or grandparent. No matter how angry you may feel about that person, your criticism of them will hurt your children and make them resent you.

By not criticising other members of your children's family, you will allow the children to feel more relaxed with you – however angry you may feel. If you have several children, they may be being looked after by different carers. This will mean they may well be missing their brothers or sisters as well as you. If there is little communication between the two homes, then make sure you pass on little items of good news about their brother or sister – nothing is too small to tell them about: a star at school, perhaps, or a new friend. Remember to tell them if their brother or sister is missing them, too.

Listening to your children

Phone calls and visits with your children are the time when you can give them the attention they need from you. Listening is one of the best gifts you can give them. Real listening, that is.

We've all experienced the occasion when we are talking to someone and we realise that they aren't really listening. How do we know? Usually it's their body language. They probably aren't engaging in any eye contact. Sometimes they interrupt with their own story or they start talking to someone else. And if you challenge them about it they usually insist they are listening. Annoying isn't it? Yet we do this all the time to our children because we think that what they are telling us isn't as important as something going on elsewhere or in our own minds.

"A mother has to be able to listen to her children and hear their views, really."

⚙ **There are several ways in which you can show your children you are listening to them:**

 ⚙ Keep eye contact while they talk to you.

 ⚙ Don't interrupt them when they are talking.

 ⚙ Don't fidget and appear distracted.

 ⚙ Really hear what they say and ask them questions about what they are telling you.

After you've had a visit or a phone call with your children it's a good idea to make notes about what they have told you: the name of their best friend, the teacher who told them off or their favourite subject. Then next time you talk to them, have your notes nearby and ask them questions about their best friend, the subjects they like and any other relevant topics.

Visits are difficult because you may have important things you need to discuss with the carer who has brought your children in to see you. However important those things are, try to keep adult discussions to a minimum while your children are within earshot. If you know that you have important things to discuss, speak quietly to the play worker or volunteer helping on the visit and ask if they could take your children off to do something in the play

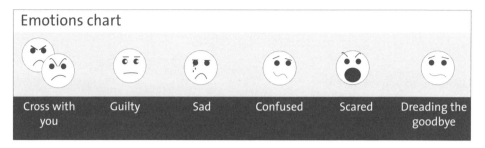

Emotions chart

Cross with you	Guilty	Sad	Confused	Scared	Dreading the goodbye

area so you can talk. The play workers and volunteers are there to help your child settle and encourage them to interact with other children. Be sensitive to the fact that they are not there to babysit.

Coping with your kids' sadness and confusion

Adults who have experienced a loved one going to prison often describe it as being like a bereavement. Children feel the same depth of sadness, but they are probably confused as well. Why does everyone think their mum is bad? Why has she left them? Why doesn't she come home? Even a month can seem like a lifetime to a child.

Older children often feel they can't upset their mother by telling them how sad they feel. They may pretend to be fine so as not to worry her. Teenagers can feel grief in the form of anger at the very person they are missing: their mother.

Don't wait for your children to express their sadness. Try to see behind negative behaviour towards you and understand that they are angry with you because they want you with them at home.

Small children find it hard to put words to their emotions. You can help them by making an emotions chart (see the top of this page) and getting them to point to the picture which best shows how they feel. However they are behaving towards you, reassure them that you love them and miss them.

Dealing with kids' nervousness

Prisons can be very scary places for children. It isn't just the fences and the clanging gates, they may have watched TV programmes about prisons and feel scared that they are filled with people who might hurt them or hurt you.

This is why you have to be so careful about reassuring your children that you are OK. Tell them about the Education course you are doing. Describe your cell to them, but call it your "bedroom" to make it sound more normal. If you have any particular friends, if possible introduce them to your children on a family day or at least tell your child about them. But be sure not to make prison sound like a cool place to be – after all you don't want your child to think that. Tell them you have to be there and you have friends there, but you'd much rather be at home.

Kids' guilt

It's not uncommon for children to feel that it is somehow their fault that their mum has gone to prison. Make it clear that it is in no way their fault. Children understand the concept of punishment for being bad, so explain that you have been sent to prison because you have broken the law. Depending on the length of your sentence and the crime involved, explain in an age-appropriate way, being as honest as you can, but sensitive.

Older children

"When I visit my cousin in prison I like it because I get to see and talk to her." 13 YEAR OLD

"I read the letters my cousin has sent to other family members." 13 YEAR OLD.

Older children may find keeping a journal helps them deal with the emotions they are going through. You can encourage this by getting them a book and maybe covering it with some nice paper from the art department.

    If you can find a project you and your children can do together, this is a great way of strengthening the bond between you. Ask them to recommend a book or TV programme and then discuss it with them. One of you could write some song lyrics and then the other could put them to music (see what musical instruments are available in the prison for you to use). Emotions are easier to express through music or a fictional character in a book or on TV.

"I wish they would let Mum out of prison."

15 year old

After your release

"Children can feel very scared. I remember when I went out on ROTL my little boy, he's four, if I go to the toilet he wants to come with me. He wants to know where I am. It's scary for them."

Tips from other mums in prison

- Take it a step at a time.

- Be prepared to compromise.

- You have to bite your tongue on occasions.

- Put your children's needs first.

- Keep positive for your children, focus on their achievements, no matter how small, and remember – it isn't forever.

- Let your children express their views, too.

- Maintain respect for other people's views.

- Try to work together – with your children's carer, the social worker, Family Engagement Worker and anyone else who may help your bond with your children.

The impact of having been separated from you for any length of time will affect your children emotionally for some while after you return home. Even just having you around again will seem strange. Some kids will be frightened you will be taken away from them again. One 8-year-old girl who had appeared to deal well with her mother going to prison for a period of months, cried when they came to fit her mother with a tag after her return home. The little girl was convinced that they had come to take her mother away again and it was the last straw for her.

Things you can do

- Book yourself in for a new hairstyle or make-over in the Education department.
- Look at what courses are on offer on Education and sign up for one.
- Look for a book on arts and crafts in the library and make something for your child's birthday or Christmas.
- Design an Emotion Chart for your child – make it age-appropriate.

- Buy notebooks and cover them with attractive paper as a journal for your childen to write in. Tell them it's a private book for them to write down how they are feeling.
- Make a wall chart with days, weeks and months for them to cross off towards your release date. Include birthdays, holidays, Christmas and family days.
- Design a certificate to give to your children as an award for something they have done well, such as helping Nan keep the house clean.

Things to take from this chapter

✓ Look after yourself. You will be able to support your children better if you are feeling well yourself.

✓ Don't suffer in silence if you are feeling low. Speak to the Family Engagement Worker, a member of the Chaplaincy staff, a Listener or tell someone you trust.

✓ Make notes to remind yourself what your children have told you, so you can ask questions next time you talk.

✓ Your children will be going through all sorts of emotions. Encourage them to talk to you about those feelings.

✓ Learn how to listen properly to your children on the phone or when they visit.

✓ Even after your return home your children will go through various emotions – be patient with them and keep listening.

✓ Don't be misled by your children apparently not being affected by your absence; older children tend to cover up their feelings, but they still need to talk them through.

CHAPTER SEVEN

Helping your children

Some mums are worried that if they tell their children's school that they are in prison, it will get round the school and local community, which may mean that other parents stop their children from playing with theirs, or that her children are bullied.

The school might find out in other ways, too. The chances are that there has been some local publicity about the case or that someone has made it their business to spread rumours.

"The school is very clear that I'm in prison. I haven't hidden anything from them."

What the school can do

"The child can become socially withdrawn, particularly if both parents are in prison."

"My little boy has been playing up at school a lot lately and I really need to be there to help, but I can't."

Schools are generally very supportive; and so they should be. Your children have done nothing wrong and deserve all the support

 ASK AN EXPERT

Educate your children's school

It's very possible that the school may not know what happens on a visit, in which case ask the **Family Engagement Worker** to ring them and talk them through the process.

CASE STUDY

One mother decided not to tell her 6-year-old daughter's school that her father had gone to prison. Several weeks into the first term, when her daughter brought her English book home, the mother was alarmed to see that on each Monday, in answer to the teacher's request: "Draw what you have done over the weekend", her daughter had carefully drawn the gates of HMP Dartmoor with her, her mother and her little brother walking through them.

they can get. If you have told the school, it will also mean that when your children visit you, the school will not assume they are bunking off and then punish them. The school can also help to prepare children for the first visit so they know what will happen; what they can or can't take in, why the dogs are there and what to expect.

 ASK AN EXPERT

Find out about your children's progress at school

Ask your kids' **school** to keep you informed of how your children are getting on and if the prison allows you to, ask if they can bring their school books in on a visit to show you what they are doing.

"I told the school I want to know what's going on with my children at school."

Communicating with the school

"It's hard. The only way that I manage to get a link to the school is if the Family Engagement Worker makes a call for me once a fortnight, where I can get updated on the kids in school."

"Unless I phone the school, I wouldn't know anything about my kids in school."

Once you are in prison you can still write and tell the school, or any other person or organisation important to your child's life, to explain what has happened. This will help them to understand what your child might be going through, and how best to support and comfort them. Speak to your Family Engagement Worker if you are nervous about what to say; they can help you to compose the letter.

The school will be more understanding if your child is grumpy or playing up at school. They will also be able to keep an eye out for any bullying of your child.

Be persistent

"S's nursery book was given to my mum when she went to the school one day, just on the off-chance. It was only 'cos she asked for it to send to me. She gave it to me when I went out on a ROTL."

You may find you have to push for contact with the school. Don't be put off if they fail to reply. Keep ringing or writing to them. Most schools are pleased when the parent takes an active

"I've been able to speak to the headmaster, the class teacher, the welfare officer, you know, but that's only because I pushed for it."

interest in their child's progress at school. Having a two-way communication with your child's teachers and the school Welfare Officer will make their task easier, too. But remember to work with them, not against them. And remember to thank anyone who has helped you in this way.

"I do have to say that the school that my kids are in, they are helpful; once or twice I've had to phone them when my little one's got issues. They did agree that every other Friday at 3 o'clock they would take the kids out of assembly so I could phone them in the office and talk to them for a couple of minutes."

Things you can do to help

You may feel that while you are in prison there is nothing you can do to help with your child's education. That's not the case. Even if your children are very little, you can make a counting book to help them learn how to count. A little later, but still pre-school, you can make an alphabet book for them.

When younger children visit you can read to them for a short while. They will love the attention and it will help them with their own reading. If you are a natural storyteller then you could start telling your children a story in episodes over the phone or on visits, finishing each episode on a cliff-hanger so that they will want to hear what happens the next time you talk, or with a joke to help them feel good just as the phone call is ending.

With older children, if they enjoy reading then ask them which book they are reading at the moment and order a copy through your prison library so you can read it, too. Then the next time they

 ASK AN EXPERT

Helping your kids with their counting or ABC

If there is a **Storybook Mum Coordinator** at the prison or a similar project, contact them and tell them you want to make a CD to go with a counting book or alphabet book. When you are doing your recording don't just read out the numbers or letters, make it more interactive by asking how many ducks they see and then pausing long enough for them to give the answer. You can ask them what noise a duck makes and again pause while they quack! This is all learning and little children love it when they can join in.

visit or you speak on the phone, you can discuss the book with them. What did they think of it? Was the ending a surprise?

Handling bullying issues

Children can be so horrible to each other and they often pick on a child who is behaving differently. We all hate the thought of our children being bullied, but it is something you need to look out for because the school will be able to take action only if it knows that the bullying is going on. If their carer, or you, have witnessed any of these behaviours (see the box below) in your children then talk to them gently – ask if everything is OK at school. They may be frightened to tell you, or they may feel you have enough to worry about already. Even little children can be very protective of their parents. Reassure your kids that you would rather know, because then you can do something about it. The child might also have been threatened by other children not to tell anyone, so be patient and tell them that the matter can be dealt with so that no one knows they told a grown-up.

> *"When I visit my mum I enjoy talking with her, telling her what I've been up to and playing basketball and badminton together."*
>
> 15 year old

Is my child being bullied?

Here are some signs that your child might be suffering from bullying:

- ❂ Not eating.
- ❂ Not wanting to go to school/bunking off school.
- ❂ Being moody.
- ❂ Wetting the bed.
- ❂ Displaying behaviour that is different from usual.

Almost everyone has had some experience of being bullied. If you were bullied you can tell your children that you know how bad they must be feeling. Try to encourage them not to fight their bully or bullies because that will only get them into more trouble. Suggest that they avoid the bullies if possible. Bullies are usually unhappy people themselves, who use fear as a way of getting others to respect them. Help your children to see that the bullies are dealing badly with their own problems. Most schools now have an anti-bullying policy and some have recruited other children to be peer mentors to bullied children.

Giving praise

We all make the mistake, at some time or other, of paying attention to our children only when they are being naughty. If they are quietly amusing themselves, we tend to leave them alone. Children want their parents' attention, so if they think the only way they can get it is by being loud and naughty, that is how they will behave.

It follows, then, that if you concentrate on praising your children when they have done something well, they will think about behaving well again. So don't use visits, phone calls or letters as an opportunity to tell your children off. Instead ask them what they have been doing and compliment them on any "good news" stories they come up with about themselves.

There may be times when you have to talk with them about some negative behaviour, but do so in a concerned way, asking why they behaved like that and what you can do to help them avoid behaving badly in future. Stress how good they are (even if they aren't!) and say how impressed you have been with them when they have done something positive.

Prison programmes on offer

Some prisons arrange for Family Learning Programmes, which enable the parent to learn together with their child.

ⓘ **Go on a computer course** in the prison because the chances are your children use computers at school and this will help you understand what they are doing on them. If they haven't learned to use computers yet, then you will be able to help them when they do.

HM Inspectorate's Expectations regarding prisoners' rights (extract)

- Prisoners are provided with verbal and written information about childcare proceedings and how to access advice services in relation to their parental rights and children's welfare.

- Prisoners who choose to represent themselves in court are given stamps and writing materials free of charge as needed to pursue their case. They have access to a computer and printer to type court correspondence and documents.

ASK AN EXPERT

Ask about parenting courses and programmes

Ask prison officials if there are any Family Learning Programmes being run at the prison you are in. Ask about parenting courses, too. You may already be an excellent parent, but we can still all learn more or refresh our ideas about our parenting skills.

If you need to write official letters to any agency or organisation or deal legally with the authorities concerning your children then the prison is legally bound to help you.

Things you can do

- Make alphabet books for your pre-school children.
- Make counting books for your small children.
- Design and make reading cards to help your children with their reading. Ask your children's teachers how best to do this, if you can.

Things to take from this chapter

✓ Contact your children's school and tell them what has happened.

✓ Ask for support from the prison's Family Engagement Worker.

✓ Focus on your children's good behaviour, reward them with praise. Offer your understanding rather than telling them off for any negative behaviour.

✓ Ask the school for regular updates on your children's progress at school and, if nothing happens, keep asking until it does.

✓ Watch out for signs of bullying and talk gently to your children if you suspect they are being bullied. If you find out that they are, tell someone at the school.

✓ Take advantage of any Family Learning or Parenting Programmes available in the prison.

CHAPTER EIGHT

Lifers are mums, too

You are still their mum

"I just take each day as it comes and concentrate on maintaining contact with my children via weekly letters and telephone contact as well as regular visits. I try not to dwell on what I have lost and what is gone but focus on what I have and what there is to look forward to with my children." MOTHER WITH 12-YEAR TARIFF

Just because you are a lifer it doesn't mean you can't be a mother to your children. Your blood still runs in their veins, your relatives are their relatives and you are still their mother. They may be angry with you, they may feel you have let them down, but they will still want to know that their mother loves them. So what can you do?

"I try and not think about all the years I will be imprisoned. I believe you go with the system, otherwise you make it harder on yourself. Being honest with officers, being polite and taking a day at a time. Do all the courses that are there for you. Have faith in yourself and show your child constant love. Rome wasn't built in a day! Good luck!" MOTHER WITH 16-YEAR TARIFF

What you can do

Here are some tips from the mother quoted above, who is serving a life sentence with a 12-year tariff:

- Focus on completing your targets.
- Be proactive.
- Always remember that if you do what is asked of you and show you are keen to change, one day you will be with your children.
- Remember that even though you are in prison you are still your children's role model and your behaviour still affects them; bad behaviour means you are away from them for longer.
- Contact your children's school and ask them to send you school reports and any other information about activities that your children are involved in.
- Your children still need you and you can still play an active role in their lives.
- Focus on what you have – not on what you have lost.

HM Inspectorate's Expectations regarding lifers & IPPs (extract)

- Prisoners who face an indeterminate sentence are identified on remand, given support and have the elements and implications of an indeterminate sentence explained to them and, where appropriate, to their families.

- Suitably trained staff explain tariffs to indeterminate sentence prisoners and, where appropriate, their families.

Let's look at seven tips from lifers who are mums

1. "Go with the system"

Prisons, like so many organisations, have to reach targets and the extract from the HM Inspector of Prisons' guidelines (above) to prisons shows that lifers and Indeterminate Public Protection (IPP) prisoners who have no fixed release date are entitled to help in understanding the implications of their sentence. Work with your Lifer Manager, Probation staff and Programmes Organiser to make the most of your time inside.

"I am blessed, as my Lifer Officer goes the extra mile and gives me positive feedback and is honest with me; no bullshit, and helps me on my black days. And I believe in him!"

"Have faith in yourself and show your child constant love."

✪ **Even if you aren't lucky with your Lifer Manager,** or you don't like the Probation staff, be polite, listen to what they have to say and show them that you can help them reach their important targets, too.

2. "Be proactive"

Instead of just waiting for someone to tell you what you must do, ask the relevant staff how you can best use your time – remember that they are expected by HM Chief Inspector of Prisons to provide you with the information you need to do this.

3. "One day you will be with your children"

If being with your children is top of your wish list, then let that be your guiding principle throughout your sentence. You may not be used to thinking before you act; that's possibly why you are in prison in the first place. Now is the time to stop and think: will this bring me closer to being with my children? Remember that negative actions will keep you from them far longer.

Ways to be proactive

- If you have a drug or alcohol problem, ask what programmes there are to help with this.

- If you need to do an offending behaviour programme, speak to the programmes officer and get your name down for it. If there is a long waiting list, write to other prisons that run the programme and if their waiting list is shorter ask to be transferred there.

- If reading or writing is a problem, go to Education and ask what courses they can offer you. Or sign up for "Toe by Toe", a project in which another prisoner will help you with your literacy problems. Then you can start writing letters to your children to tell them how much you love them. And you can read their replies in private, without having to ask someone else to read them for you.

- If you have always wanted to be a hairdresser or study law, now is the time to look into relevant courses you can do in prison – you've got the time, after all.

- Find out about family days and get your name down for the next one you are eligible for as soon as possible.

- Find out if your prison provides a "Story CD" project – it doesn't matter if your reading isn't good, they can edit out any mistakes you might make and it will mean your child will be able to listen to your voice whenever they want.

- If your family is too far away to visit you, find out if you can be transferred to a prison which is closer to them. If not, then ask about accumulated visits where you can be transferred temporarily to another prison for a bank of time for visits from your family.

 ASK AN EXPERT

Putting together a plan for your future

From the start of your sentence it's worth asking for help from staff to put together a plan that will show you are taking your future and rehabilitation seriously. If possible, involve your family in the planning stage. Notice that the HM Inspectorate's guidelines ask that the sentence is explained to the family as well, where possible (see page 61). Your family may be key to the success of your plan and they will want to understand and contribute to it as well. Your **Family Engagement Worker** can help with this link.

Nor do you want to become a stranger to your children, so keep regular contact – weekly letters, phone calls and visits if they are near enough. Make cards for their birthdays, Christmas and other special occasions and congratulate them when they do well at school or achieve a milestone.

Sign up for any projects that might strengthen the bond with your children and help you be a great mother to them.

4. "You are still their role model"

Don't think that because you have made a horrendous mistake that means you can't be a good role model for your child. How you deal with the consequences of your offence and the time you spend in prison will have a deep effect on your child.

✪ **If you are constantly kicking off** and trying to buck the system, kept in high security and refusing to do any programmes, your child will read this as you not wanting to come back home.

Small children look up to their parents and try to be like them. Even though you are not living with your child, they will want to be like you. If you don't want your children to be constantly in trouble and deprived of privileges that other children get, then you have to behave well in order to set them a good example.

If you want your children to be honest with you, you have to show them by example and be honest with them. Of course you need to be sensitive to their ages and what they can understand, but don't build unrealistic hopes for them; it will only lead to disappointment and a lack of trust.

"They understand that release will happen when a parole board sits and they are satisfied that I am no longer a risk. My children have always known what happened and have read what the newspapers wrote. They say they do not feel any different towards me. Often they ask questions which I try to answer if I am able to."

✪ **Everyone makes mistakes** and you are no exception, so admit your mistakes and show your children how you can learn from them.

5. "You can still play an active part in your kids' lives"

Providing you are allowed contact with your children then there is no reason for a school to refuse to send you their reports and answer your questions about their progress. Even if your tariff means you won't be out of prison until after your child has left school, don't feel that this excludes you from taking an active part in their education.

6. "Focus on what you already have"

You may be separated from your children, but if you are allowed contact you can still be part of their lives and remember that guiding principle: one day you will be with your children again.

" I am in contact with the headmaster and receive all their school reports."

Be sure to ...

- Ask your children what their favourite subjects are.
- Ask them what projects they are doing at school and if it is something you can help them with by looking for information in the prison library – then offer to help them.
- Discuss their subjects with them and be prepared to admit that they have learned something you didn't know.
- Share the excitement of learning with them by taking a course yourself which they might be interested in and letting them know how you are getting on.
- Read the same book as them, so you can discuss it on the phone or at the next visit.

✪ **Make the most of your phone calls and their visits.** Plan for them and keep them positive. Enjoy your kids' company instead of dwelling on the parting to come at the end of the day. By keeping positive you will help them to stay strong, too.

Resist the temptation to blame circumstances or other people, however justified you think this might be. Life throws a lot of rubbish at us sometimes and we are judged by how we deal with those difficulties.

7. "Show your children constant love"

"When I visit my Mummy I enjoy face-painting, cuddles, everything, playing together." 5 YEAR OLD

"I enjoy getting to give her cuddles and kisses and playing basketball on family day." 11 YEAR OLD

"Communication – by telephone, letters and knowing I am OK and me knowing my children are staying strong."

Your family are your public face. While you are in prison the walls may keep you there, but they also act as a barrier to the stigma and bad publicity that may be attached to your offence. Your family don't have this protection and will need your help to stay strong in the face of any negative criticism or accusations they may suffer on your behalf.

Your children will want to believe you rather than the people who are criticising you, so by showing your children the love and understanding they need and deserve, you will be proving that you are not such a bad person as some people like to make out.

> *" I enjoy cuddle time with Mummy when I visit."*
>
> 20 month old

Rome wasn't built in a day

You have a huge challenge ahead of you and no one is expecting you to be perfect. Remember the quote at the beginning of this chapter in which the woman with a tariff of 12 years says she takes each day as it comes and concentrates on maintaining contact with her children (see page 60).

Your family, particularly your children, will be confused by the system and won't understand the terms. Be patient with them and explain how the system works. Prepare them for delays and disappointments.

ASK AN EXPERT

Parole reviews

Ask the **Family Engagement Worker** to explain to your family, too that delays don't necessarily mean you aren't doing all you can to get out as early as possible. Parole reviews are frequently deferred or delayed and this can be bitterly disappointing for you. They are disappointing for your children, too because they want you home again; to a certain extent their life is on hold as well.

The "stays" that will support you

Just like a Victorian lady's corset, there are stays that will support you:

- Stay busy.
- Stay active.
- Stay in touch with your children.
- Stay positive.
- Stay proactive.
- Stay fit.
- Stay focused.
- Stay cool!

By dealing well with those disappointments and delays you will not only demonstrate to your Offender Manager that you can deal with challenges, it will be an excellent example to your children on how best to handle their disappointments in life.

If you are not in contact with your children

There are still things you can do for them. Remember that you are their birth mother and they will, in time, want to know more about you and your family. Think about creating a memory box (see below) for them which you can add to and make available to them when they are older.

Make a memory box

Some things which could go into a memory box – check with social services what items you will be allowed to include.

- A photo of you. If you have one of your kids when they were babies, then so much the better.
- A photo of you when you were little – so they can spot family likenesses.
- A photo of you on a positive occasion – collecting a prize at school or enjoying a day out with your family.
- A letter from you telling them that, although you are in prison now, you will always love them.
- Something about your kids' family history. It doesn't have to be a full family tree, but if you had a parent or grandparent who was particularly kind or did something special, describe them and what they did that was so good.
- Things you have made for them like a story CD, a soft toy, a notebook for them to write in and birthday cards.

Things you can do

- **Write up your wish list**, take out the unrealistic wishes and add those which are achievable.
- **Design a "stays" poster** for your wall, listing the "stays" that will help you get through (see facing page).
- **Start planning a memory box** – even if you do have contact with your children, a memory box will be something for them to enjoy when they are older.
- **Design a scrapbook**, marking the positive things that have happened to you in your life and which you still have souvenirs of – like letters from your children, photos, funny things that have happened.
- **Write a story** for your child and then ask to make it into a story CD for them.

Things to take from this chapter

✓ Being a lifer doesn't stop you from being a good mother.

✓ Prisons are expected to ensure that families of people with indeterminate sentences are helped to understand the consequences of their tariffs.

✓ Good behaviour will get you back with your children sooner than bad behaviour.

✓ Prison staff have targets to meet; by helping you, you can help them to reach these targets.

✓ Don't lose sight of your own target – one day you will be with your children.

✓ Be politely persistent in getting help and support with your plans.

✓ You can still be a positive role model for your children while you are in prison.

✓ If you aren't allowed contact with your children you can create a memory box for them.

✓ You can still take an active part in their development and education.

✓ Your children need to know you love them – constantly remind them of this.

✓ Don't give up hope – be patient and you will get through.

CHAPTER NINE

Preparing for release

> "It's going to be easy for a child to think, 'Hold on a minute, why are you coming back into my life? Where have you been for the last year or so?'"

Coming up to release is an exciting time. You can't wait to be back with your children and you have all sorts of plans; things you will do together, places you will visit and, above all, being a much better parent – to make up for all the grief and separation you have put your kids through. It's going to be sweet. But it's also a scary time because of what might have been going on while you were in prison.

Before release

Even with long sentences, preparation for release needs to start at the beginning of your time in prison. That way you can make the best of your time inside, making it relevant to what you want out of life when you are released. We have talked about the importance of keeping in touch with your children and their carer (see chapter 2). That must be number one on your list of important things to do. A child who doesn't hear from their parent will always think it is because that parent doesn't care for them. They see you as ignoring them and you can't "ignore" them for a period of time and then suddenly be keen to talk to them or see them. They will be confused and angry.

Once you have set up a good channel of communication with your children, whether through letters, phone calls or visits, the next task is to think about what you need to do while in prison to help you be as good a mum as you can be when you are released. By keeping focused on this you will help the time go by quicker. You will also impress the officers and that always helps towards being released as early as possible.

> "He now knows who I am, due to me going out and spending days with him."

Release on Temporary Licence (ROTL)

"I'm at the stage now in my sentence where I go out on ROTL once every 28 days. I've had overnights, things like that."

Providing you are not one of the following, you may qualify for release on temporary licence:

♻ Category A prisoner.

- Prisoner on the escape list.
- Prisoner who is subject to extradition proceedings.
- Remand and convicted unsentenced prisoner.
- Sentenced prisoner who is remanded for further charges or further sentencing.
- Prisoner held on behalf of the International Criminal Tribunal for the Former Yugoslavia (ICTY), the Special Court for Sierra Leone (SCLS) or the International Criminal Court (ICC).

There are four types of ROTL and these are explained in the table on page 70.

- Resettlement Day Release (RDR).
- Resettlement Overnight Release (ROR).
- Childcare Resettlement Licence (CRL).
- Special Purpose Licence (SPL).

Release on Temporary Licence (or as it is always known, ROTL) is a way of helping you keep your bond strong with your children.

 ASK AN EXPERT

What are the current rules about ROTL?

The system in UK prisons is constantly changing and the rules and types of ROTL are bound to change as well, particularly with the introduction of resettlement prisons. So ask the **Family Engagement Worker** to explain what the current rules are about ROTL and whether or not you would be able to apply for it.

⚙ **Whatever the rules, applications for ROTL take a long time to be processed**. Sometimes they get lost. At the beginning ask how long you might have to wait before you are given a decision. Do keep asking where yours is in the process.

Try not to get too excited, because the authorities will always consider any risks of adverse publicity which might be attracted if they are seen as letting someone out of prison who is still a danger to society or who may cause their victim distress. Don't tell

Release on Temporary Licence (ROTL)

Types	Who can apply?	What for?	Frequency	Duration	Considerations
Resettlement Day Release (RDR)	• All eligible prisoners depending on length of sentence served. • Prisoners on recall. • Prisoners granted Home Detention Curfew (HDC).	• Community/unpaid work as part of sentence. • Training/education. • Maintaining family ties. • Housing. • Probation interviews. • Job searches/interviews. • Opening bank accounts.			According to result of risk assessment.
Resettlement Overnight Release (ROR)	• Category D prisoners. • Resettlement prisoners. • Prisoners with a Parole Eligibility Date (PED). • Some Category C prisoners.	• To spend time at their release address. • To re-establish links with family and local community. • To attend interviews for work, training or accommodation.	Governor decides but not usually more than four nights.		According to: • Risk assessment. • How close to release. • Parole process. • Parole Eligibility Date.
Childcare Resettlement Licence (CRL)	Eligible prisoners with sole caring responsibility for child under 16.	• To retain tie with child. • To prepare for resuming parental duties on release. • To help the child deal with separation.	No more than once every two months.	No more than three nights at a time.	According to: • Proof of sole carer status. • Risk assessment. • Permission of temporary carer if at their home. • No risk to victim's well-being.
Special Purpose Licence (SPL)	• All eligible prisoners. • Prisoners with parental responsibility for child under 16.	• Visits to dying relatives. • Funerals. • Tragic personal circumstances. • To deal with emergency relating to their caring duties. • Sole carers of elderly or severely disabled relative to deal with emergency relating to their duties.	Few hours to achieve purpose. Governor has discretion to allow over-night absence.	Up to four nights in any one calendar month.	According to: • Normal risk assessment. • Home circumstances report. • Victim issues where appropriate. • Wish of relative to see the prisoner.

your children you may be coming home until your ROTL has been approved in writing. If you tell their carer when you first apply, make absolutely sure they don't let the cat out of the bag and tell your children. You don't want your children getting all excited, only to hear that Mum isn't coming home early after all.

Your children's lives while you have been away

Your children have had to adapt because however close their carer is to you, they will have been doing things differently for, and with, your children. Here are some examples that mothers have found:
- Their children's hair hasn't been cut the same way as before.
- They have been dressed in old-fashioned clothes.
- Their diet has been different.
- They have been left on their own, despite being young.
- They haven't been allowed to see their mum's family.
- The mum's religious/cultural beliefs have not been respected.

You may have had more frightening concerns, such as knowing that drugs have been in the house where your child has lived, the carer is alcoholic or even violent. If this is the case, you are probably viewing your release with a certain amount of dread. Instead of sitting and worrying about it, it's time to do what you can to prepare for your release.

 ASK AN EXPERT

If you are worried about your kids

If you have any concerns about your children's lives in your absence it is really important to speak to the **Family Engagement Worker**, your personal officer, the Prison Public Protection Unit or your social worker so action can be taken to protect your children, if necessary.

Access to your child

If you are not being released to the family home where your child lives, you need to get access to your child. As soon as you can, speak to the social workers, the family solicitor (and anyone else) to establish what contact you are allowed.

If a Court Order is required, the sooner you start proceedings the better. You may wish to go to court to reverse a Residency Order that was set up while you were in prison. All this takes time.

"This is the hardest sentence I've ever done because I know what I've got and what I've been missing out on."

If Probation are insisting you go to a hostel first, be aware that you will probably not be allowed to have your children visit the hostel or to stay overnight (although you can see them elsewhere). Prepare your children and reassure them that as soon as you are able to find a place to live, they will come and live with you – if it is allowed. Don't make any promises you may not be able to deliver.

Changes

Changes will have taken place in everyone concerned. Here are some that may have happened to you:

- Your outlook on life may have altered; you've "grown up".
- You've had a wake-up call and want to do things differently in the future.
- You appreciate the things you had since you've been away from them more.
- You have made new friendships while you've been in prison.
- You may have gained qualifications that you want to use to find work outside.
- You may want to build on the education you have had in prison by going to college.
- You may have arranged to go to rehab to sort out any addictions you might have.
- You may be feeling very angry about something that has gone on while you have been in prison.

Life hasn't stood still for your children either since you have been away. Although you have kept in touch and had visits, you will notice the changes in them even more when you are released:

- They will have got older.
- Their behaviour may have lacked boundaries while you were away, so they may play up more when returned to your care.
- They will have achieved milestones in their development – walking, talking or starting school, for example.
- Their personalities will have developed.
- Their interests will have changed.
- They will have developed new friendships.
- They will have formed bonds with other people, particularly their carer.

Don't forget the impact your imprisonment has had on your children and family members, too; they will have had to change.

"I know I won't re-offend because of how hard this sentence has been. I've missed out 17 months of my little boy's life."

They are probably stressed and, for example, grandparents may seem older now. On top of this, their trust in you may have broken down. They will have had to get by without you, too, so they have taken on new roles and when you join them again you may feel you have no role to play in the family yourself. This is natural and it's vital to take things slowly, gradually offering to take on roles that will ease the burden on the rest of the family.

So how do you deal with these changes? Here are some ideas put forward by other mothers who have been through this experience:

- If a grandmother has been your children's main carer, allow her to take a step back and just be a nan again. One of the joys of being a grandparent is being able to hand the children back when you're tired or if they are getting difficult.
- If the bond between your children and their carer is particularly strong, when the children are back with you, take them to see the carer as often as possible. If they live too far away then let the children phone them.
- Suggest the children make a special card for the carer on the carer's birthday or at Christmas.
- Send the carer photos of the children. Just as you loved getting photos of them while you were separated from them, so will the carer, who has formed a strong bond with your children.
- Take things gradually. You have all been through a tremendous upheaval, both practically and emotionally. Don't just expect to pick up where you left off.
- Congratulate yourself when you are able to deal well with a difficult situation.
- Don't beat yourself up if you fail. Take a deep breath, apologise and move on.

"It would be easy for a mother that gets out of prison with all that guilt they've got for not being there for them, to buy their kid lots of stuff. But you can't do that."

One of the things the mothers who helped to write this book said several times was that you can't buy love. You have to show your love through giving your children your time, your attention and your love. That is worth far more than expensive presents.

Setting boundaries

"You have to be there emotionally for them as well, but giving them boundaries too. You have to understand that it's going to be hard for your child to know why all of a sudden they've got these boundaries. But they still need them."

"Be consistent with your child. But also at the same time you have to set boundaries."

In order for your children and you to develop a good relationship with each other again there has to be some work on the ground rules. Children need to have realistic, firm boundaries. Periodically, as they advance and develop, they try to push those boundaries and sometimes these need to be reset to take account of the children's development.

To be effective, ground rules must have a reason behind them. When children challenge a rule, you have to be able to explain why the rule has been established. "Because I say so" is a very tempting response, but it's not good enough for children. You may not have time to explain each rule every time they complain, but tell them you will explain when you have more time – for now, they just need to follow the rule.

It is very likely that the boundaries set by the children's carer are different from the ones you want to establish. If the children are old enough to have a conversation with you, when you have some time at the beginning of your new relationship with them, sit down with them and suggest you draw up some ground rules together. Discuss each one in turn and ask if they feel there are any that you have left out. If they come up with an unrealistic rule like "I am allowed to go to bed whenever I want", explain to them why that rule isn't going to work.

They may like to set some ground rules for you, such as "no smoking in the house" or "no swearing". You may not like this idea, but if it sounds like a good rule then include it and allow them to tell you off if you disregard the rule later. After all, they may well point out that you were in prison because you broke the law.

Getting into a routine

By establishing a routine in your life outside prison you will give it a solid structure, which will help your child to feel more stable and protected. Be realistic about your routine. Don't expect either you or your children to stick to a rigid or demanding routine. Give yourself some leeway, but above all, stay strong.

How to turn your life around

Here are suggestions from mothers in prison as to how you can break the cycle that may have got you into prison in the first place:

- Stay clean.
- Build positive relationships.
- Seek good support.
- Take each day as it comes – if you are an addict you are always in recovery, so stay strong and keep yourself safe.
- Relocate to avoid people who are a bad influence on you.

A breakdown can be a breakthrough

A breakdown in family links may seem overwhelming, but sometimes it is the shake-up you and your family have needed in order to reach a better understanding and deeper relationship with each other. Often family relationships improve while a member is in prison, addressing their addiction or behavioural problems. This provides everyone with a firmer foundation from which to build your new life.

"A mother has to have patience, particularly if she has got more children and if one has learning difficulties or behaviour problems."

Be honest with yourself about what qualities you will need to deal with the difficulties you face when you are released. Here is a list of qualities which mothers in prison say you need when you are released:

- Respect for other people's views.
- Understanding.
- Patience.
- Good listening skills.
- Stability.
- Sensitivity to the needs of others.
- Honesty.
- Tolerance.

" A mother has got to be reliable, she's got to be there for her kids."

This may seem like quite a list. However, no one is expecting you to be a perfect mother – no such thing exists. You need to be realistic about your own stress levels. When you lose your patience or fail to tolerate someone else's behaviour, apologise and explain that you are feeling stressed and explain why. Even if you have to do this with a young child, explain everything in simple terms.

Don't focus on your failings. At the end of each day run through the list of qualities you need to acquire and tick off the occasions during the day when you have used them. Give yourself a pat on the back for your successes.

Rebuilding trust

"I get it from my mum, she says 'Oh I don't know, what's different this time?' At the end of the day you can't blame them for thinking like that. Don't be put off by the comments they make to you. You can do it if you put your mind to it. You're a mother, you've got no choice."

"*You've just got to prove it. You've just got to take what they're saying, don't get angry.*"

Your family may be pleased that you have, for example, come off the drugs while you've been in prison. You are probably looking much healthier and they can hold a sensible conversation with you. But that's not enough. If they've seen you like this before but watched you slide back into your old ways, they are bound to question what is different this time. Be patient with them and be prepared to prove to them, again and again, that you really have changed for the better.

✪ **They won't trust you overnight,** but if you consistently stick to your new regime, little by little over time they will start to believe that you can do it this time.

If you want to be with your children as they grow up, you have no choice but to keep on treading your new path.

"*Arrange to do something for yourself so you can be a better parent for your child.*"

Because you're worth it

"At the same time, when you're out, you need to have some time for yourself, when the kids are in bed. That's why it's important to have a routine."

In your eagerness to be a good mother to your children, the perfect partner, a reformed daughter for your parents and a loving sister for your siblings, don't forget to look after yourself, too. You can be none of those things if you are feeling tired or depressed, if your self-esteem is low and if you feel you can't cope with the outside world.

Explain to your family that you will need some time to build up your reserves of strength and need to set aside some time each day to do something that helps this process. Be firm but realistic about this. Your family will understand if you say you need an hour or two in the evenings to relax and enjoy life. If you say you can spare them two hours of the day but the rest of the time you'll be out with your mates... guess what, they probably won't be very supportive! (See the box below for guidelines for keeping prisoners' links with their families strong.)

HM Inspectorate's Expectations – children, families and contact with the outside world (extract)

17. Prisoners are encouraged to re-establish or maintain relationships with their children and families where it is appropriate.

- Prisoners' distance from home, frequency of visits, parental status and, where applicable, number of dependants are established on arrival and monitored thereafter.
- There is adequate provision of accumulated visits and children/family days to meet the needs of the population.
- Arrangements for receiving additional visits from children or immediate family members are in place and there is provision to receive incoming calls from children, or to deal with arrangements for children.
- Efforts are made to assist prisoners who have family living far away to maintain good family contact.
- Where appropriate, families are encouraged to be involved in supporting prisoners, such as during resettlement planning and care and support plan (ACCT) reviews.
- There is a qualified family support worker in place to help prisoners to maintain contact with their children, fulfil their parental responsibilities or to support those undergoing separation and child protection procedures.
- Primary carers are provided with additional free letters and phone calls, and are able to receive incoming calls from dependants.
- Release on Temporary Licence is used appropriately to help maintain contact with dependants, and where release on licence is unsuitable, in-house arrangements are made, where appropriate, for extended pre-release contact with children and families.
- General relationship counselling for prisoners and their immediate family members is available, and prisoners have access to programmes/interventions for improving parenting skills and relationships.
- Staff working in these areas have good links with all relevant staff working with prisoners and, where applicable, services contribute to meeting sentence/custody plan targets.

Things you can do

How well do you know your children now?

- **Make a list** of your children's favourite things: colours, stories, films, food and toys.
- **What are the names** of your children's best friends?
- **What do they like best** about school?
- **What do they like least** about school?
- **What do they want to be** when they grow up?
- **What are their favourite hobbies** and pastimes?

When you speak to your children see how many of these you have got right. Keep a note and ask them again in six months' time.

A couple of other things you could do:

- **Make a list of what you need to do** to prepare for your release.
- **Draw up a list of what you want to achieve** and match it with an action list.

Things to take from this chapter

✓ Start preparing for release at the beginning of your sentence, whatever length that sentence may be.

✓ Nothing stands still. Consider the changes that have taken place in you, your children, your family and in the outside world.

✓ When you are released develop a routine for your kids and stick to it as much as possible.

✓ Find out as much as you can about your children's lives while you are in prison, so there isn't a big gap in your knowledge. Keep in contact with them right from the start of your sentence.

✓ Ask about Release on Temporary Licence (ROTL) and apply for it if you can. Be prepared to wait for the decision, and perhaps to be disappointed. Don't let your child know until ROTL is approved.

✓ Your relationships with your family will be different, but they can be better if you are honest with each other and with yourself.

✓ Read the guidelines laid down by HM Inspectorate of Prisons to maintain and improve prisoners' relationships with their children and families.

✓ Don't forget to look after yourself, too. Find good support and use it. A happy mother is a better mother.

✓ Find out what access you will have to your children on release and prepare accordingly.

✓ Rebuilding trust with your family will take a long time. Be patient with them. You will have to constantly prove to them that you have changed before they will really start to relax.

✓ Your children need boundaries. Decide on the ground rules for when you are released and then stick to them. Discuss them with your children and family if you can.

✓ Be determined to break the cycle of crime by remaining strong and staying away from people who have a negative influence on you.

CHAPTER TEN

The vicious circle

Dealing with your own experiences

As you can see from the extract from HM Inspectorate of Prison guidelines (see box below), it is very important for anyone who has been a victim of abuse to receive support to prevent this vicious circle from repeating itself after release from prison.

In order to be the best mum you can be, you need to feel you are in control of your life. If someone else is causing you harm or trying to control you, this will affect your ability to give your own children the love and guidance they need.

It may be the case that you suffered abuse as a child: physical, mental, sexual abuse – or all three. You may feel this is now in the past, but if you've done nothing to address the legacy of emotions that the experience has left, it could still affect your mothering skills now.

HM Inspectorate's Expectations – additional resettlement services (extract)

21. Prisoners who have been the victim of abuse, rape or domestic violence are identified and supported to address their specific needs.

- Prisoners are able to disclose their experience of domestic violence, rape or abuse promptly after arrival. The environment and staff show sensitivity to prisoners disclosing such information.
- There are specific interventions available, such as counselling services and accredited programmes, delivered in groups or one to one.
- Activities in the regime help to build the confidence levels and coping skills of prisoners who have disclosed abuse, rape or domestic violence.

- Prisoners receive information on the support available to them in the community and have access to legal information.
- Prison staff are aware of associated safety risks to the prisoners and, where applicable, their children, and relevant information is shared securely with other agencies in the community.
- Prison staff work closely with external organisations to address the range of resettlement support needs of prisoners who have experienced abuse, rape or domestic violence.

ASK AN EXPERT

Dealing with abuse

Addressing your own abuse is not something you can do without help. If you are worried about confidentiality then speak to a **Listener**. There is also a list of helplines specifically for victims of abuse at the end of this book (see page 94). Speak to your **Family Engagement Worker,** too, because they will know what support is available, both inside and out of the prison. Ask them about pattern-changing programmes, safety planning and assertiveness programmes available in the establishment. A prison sentence does give you time to address issues, so if you want something positive to come out of what appears to be a very negative experience, use your time in prison to get the help you need, so that you don't leave prison and find yourself back in a vicious circle of abuse.

ASK AN EXPERT

If the abuse doesn't stop

Being in prison doesn't necessarily mean the abuse will stop. It can continue through phone calls and if the abuser has care of your children, it may be that they are using that to control you. There are things that can be done to prevent this. Phone calls can be monitored, professionals can provide support and advice or even take action, and phone numbers can be blocked by the prison. Please speak to your **Family Engagement Worker**, someone on the **Chaplaincy** staff or another **staff member** you feel you can trust.

The poison in the post

Prisons can be lonely places and letters from friends or family are life-savers, helping you to get through your sentence. They can even be the start of a new relationship if you have struck up a correspondence with someone you don't know through Jail Mail or Royal Mail, or maybe someone you once knew a long time ago.

These letters may be from someone with good intentions, but they can also be a means of reaching vulnerable women for controlling or manipulative people. Furthermore, they can be the first step for a paedophile grooming you, in order to gain access to your children. So tread warily. Show the letters to someone you trust and ask for their honest opinion of them. If the contact has moved on to making telephone calls to you, ask a friend to stand nearby so that if you are being threatened or asked to do something you don't want to do they can listen in.

⚙ **Tempting though it may be to keep a new and exciting relationship private,** just to be sure, do tell someone you trust about it.

Protecting your child

It may be that your children are being cared for, or have contact with, the perpetrator of your own abuse and you are terrified that they may also experience violence at their hands.

If your children can't visit because of the distance or lack of carer to bring them in to see you, providing they are not legally prevented from having contact with your child, your family can fight for access if the carer is preventing them from any contact.

 ASK AN EXPERT

If you have concerns about your children's safety

When you see your children you can use the emotions chart in Chapter 6 (see page 50) to assess how they are feeling at home. If you have concerns about your children's safety and happiness, don't wade in with accusations, however tempted you may be, instead speak to your **Family Engagement Worker** or **another staff member**, who can help you to take your concerns further.

You can ring **Childline** if you have concerns about your children's safety; it's not just a helpline for children to ring. You can also contact the appropriate **Child Assessment Framework (CAF) person** from the area where your child is living and let them know about your concerns. The child's school will be able to find out who the CAF person is and what their contact details are.

If your children's carer is not bringing them to see you

As long as you are legally allowed contact with your children, if for some reason their carer is not bringing them in to see you, then you should ask for supervised contact. This may involve you having to get your **solicitor** onto the case and if you are worried that you can't afford it you can apply for **Legal Aid**.

ASK AN EXPERT

Before you lash out

It is very important to seek help from professionals you can trust before you reach the point of lashing out. There are a couple of case studies (see page 84) where the **Open project,** which offers support for women offenders in Devon and Cornwall, was able to help women tackle their offending, abuse experiences and behaviour patterns. Open is just one of the programmes offered nationally to support women offenders who have suffered abuse and domestic violence.

Paying the price for hitting back

It's possible that you are in prison precisely because you have tried to stop the abuse through using violence yourself. After years of submission, you may have finally cracked and lashed out, with frightening consequences.

. . . .

✪ If you haven't yet, but you're tempted...don't!

. . . .

Using violence to prevent violence will affect the support you are entitled to. Some support agencies won't work with women who have violent convictions. This is because they have to protect other clients and their staff. Furthermore, perpetrators often know that if they report violence on behalf of the victim to an agency before the victim, then the agency will support the perpetrator rather than the victim – a kind of dark "first come, first served" situation.

CASE STUDY Patsy

Patsy was in prison for supplying Class A and B drugs. She had served one year of her two-year sentence and was due for release, provided suitable accommodation could be found for her in Exeter that would cater for her mobility difficulties. She was referred to Open.

During her first meeting with her Open support worker, Patsy revealed that she had been the victim of domestic violence and childhood abuse, which led to her alcohol and substance misuse, offending and generally chaotic lifestyle.

Her Open support worker was able to arrange for temporary accommodation with a relative, so that she could be released from prison. Not only was her support worker active in helping her apply for housing and search for suitable education and training, she was also able to gain Patsy's trust so that she felt she had someone there to help her in her ultimate aim of one day regaining contact with her three children, who had been taken into care.

CASE STUDY Cathy

Cathy was a prolific offender who was referred to Open because she had breached a court order and re-offended, causing assault and damage to another person's property while under the influence of alcohol and drugs.

Her Open support worker advised her to apply for a Female Offender Specified Activity Requirement Order (FOSAR) and provided her with the relevant information to present to her solicitor and Probation.

Cathy discussed with her Open support worker her needs, including work on relationships and safety planning to address her recurring history of being a victim of domestic violence. Working with her support worker, she managed to avoid a prison sentence, complete her FOSAR, cut down on her alcohol consumption, stop her street drug abuse and regain care of her son.

She did an important part of the work with her Open support worker, addressing her experience of abuse from family members during her childhood and from partners later on. She felt that if she had been able to do this work sooner, she might not have got into such deep trouble.

Things to take from this chapter

✓ Prisons are expected to provide good support for victims of domestic abuse.

✓ It is very important to deal with any experiences of abuse you may have suffered yourself in the past. Being able to understand and deal with those experiences, even if they have now ended, will help you to feel in control of your life in future.

✓ If you suspect your children may be the victim of abuse or are potentially at risk, speak to your Family Engagement Worker, personal officer, Chaplaincy staff or Prison Public Protection Unit and seek their guidance and support.

✓ Some abusers can use Jail Mail to seek out and manipulate victims, so be careful with any new relationships you form, even postal ones.

✓ Seek professional help rather than hit back, however angry you may feel with your abuser. Otherwise, if you take revenge you may seriously affect your own rights and support.

Things I need to remember ...

Arrangements for your children: legal options

Bridget Lindley & Mary Stephenson

With luck, you have been able to arrange for your children to be cared for by their father or other family members who share your parenting ideas and will put what is best for your children first. This means you can work together as a family to help your children cope with the separation from you, to keep in touch with you and Children's Services don't have to get involved. Sadly this is not always the case. If you have not been able to make family arrangements or there are other concerns about your children's welfare, Children's Services may have to be involved.

Experiences of Children's Services and the care system vary from case to case; some are negative and some positive. In prison, you sometimes hear horrendous stories about children being taken from their families by Children's Services. You may also be worried about whether your children are being cared for properly. This section is designed to help you understand the child welfare system, what Children's Services can and cannot do and how you can ensure the best for your children while you are in prison. However, this is not a substitute for you getting advice about your own case. Ask the prison staff to help you get this advice – see page 94 for details of helplines and how to contact a solicitor who specialises in children's law.

When do Children's Services get involved?

Children's Services are not automatically called in when a mother goes to prison. You can make your own arrangements with someone you think is suitable to care for your children if there is a chance you might go to prison. Planning ahead is good, so you can set this up before you go to court. Children's Services are not normally involved unless:

- They think the arrangements you have made are not suitable and may place your children at risk **or**
- You have made a private fostering arrangement. This is when the person you arrange to care for your children is not their grandparent, aunt, uncle, sibling or step-parent, or a local authority foster-carer, and the arrangement is likely to be for more than 28 days. If it is

a private fostering arrangement, Children's Services will need to be informed (see page 91).

If you have to take your children with you when you appear in court, and there is no trustworthy relative going with you (who is willing to look after your children should you be sent to prison), then Children's Services will be called in to arrange their temporary care. You may be asked to sign a Section 20 agreement allowing your children to be looked after in the care system. It is extremely important that you get specialist legal advice about whether you should sign this form. If you have not been able to get this advice before signing this agreement, ask the prison staff to help you contact a solicitor once you get to prison. If you don't sign the agreement, Children's Services may apply to court for a Care Order, which allows them to take your children into care, even if you don't agree. You need to speak to a solicitor or a specialist adviser as soon as possible.

If you have not taken your children to court with you, Children's Services might still become involved if they receive a referral from another person saying that they should investigate your children's needs. These referrals are likely to be from a member of your family, your children's school, a health visitor or a neighbour who is concerned about your children.

What Children's Services can and cannot do
Child protection

If Children's Services receive information that makes them concerned about your children, for example that they are living with someone who might be putting them at risk, they must carry out a child-protection investigation (or make child-protection enquiries), including an assessment of your children's circumstances. If their worries are confirmed after they have made enquires, they may hold a child-protection conference to decide if a plan is needed. This plan would set out what action is required in order to keep your children safe, including what help would be given to your children and their carer.

You should normally be involved in this assessment

and in drawing up a plan, but this can be difficult if you are in prison. However, it is still important that you tell the social worker your views. Ask the prison staff to help you send a letter to the social worker telling them your views and what you want for your children. It is also very important that you ask members of your family and/or friends who could help care for your children, to contact the social worker and ask to be involved in making plans.

Removing children into the care system

Your children can only be taken into care if you or someone else who has parental responsibility for them agrees or the court makes a Care Order saying they can be taken into care long-term, or it makes an Interim Care Order, saying that they are in care temporarily. In order for a local authority to obtain a Care Order or Interim Care Order to enable them to remove children, there are very specific grounds that the local authority has to establish. You should be involved in the care proceedings and have a right to free legal aid, so ask the prison staff as soon as possible to help you find a specialist solicitor to represent you.

If there is an emergency and your children suddenly need to be taken into care, social services might apply to court for an Emergency Protection Order, saying your children can be removed into care for up to eight days. This can be extended once for a further seven days. After that, Children's Services have to start care proceedings if they want to keep your children in care.

If the situation is so urgent that Children's Services don't have time to apply to court for an Emergency Protection Order, they can ask the police to take your children into police protection. This means that the police can take your children to a safe place for up to 72 hours. If they do this they must contact Children's Services, who will take over responsibility for arranging care for them.

Involve your wider family

If your children are taken into care, Children's Services should first consider placing them with their other parent (subject to assessment). If the other parent is not considered suitable, then they should explore placing them with other relatives, who are assessed by the social worker as being suitable and are approved as foster-carers.

You should therefore ask your children's other parent, and anyone in your family you trust to raise your children who you think is willing and able to take on their care, to get in touch with a social worker and ask to be assessed. If they are approved as a foster-carer for your children, they have a right to apply for support for your children, if necessary.

There is a range of different **legal routes for relatives** or friends to take on the care of your children, with differing types of support available, including:
- Your children are looked after by Children's Services either under a Care Order, an Emergency Protection Order or in accommodation by agreement with you/the other parent/others with parental responsibility. The children are then placed with your relative/friend, who must be assessed and approved as a foster-carer. This carer has a right to financial and other support to raise your children and they can be prioritised for places in local schools, if necessary.
- Your relatives/friends apply to court for a Child Arrangements Order (saying that the children will live with them) or a Special Guardianship Order. These orders give them the possibility of getting financial and other support (for example for buying beds or locating a child-minder) from the local authority, depending on individual assessment.
- You and your friends/relatives make a private arrangement and there is no court or Children's Services' involvement, in which case the carer can only get financial and other support (as above) if your children are assessed by the social worker as being "in need".

It is important that a potential family member or friend who is considering taking on the care of your children understands all the legal options that are open to them. So it is a good idea for you to tell them that they should get specialist independent advice immediately – there are helplines they can contact (see page 94) or they may want to see their own specialist solicitor. It is important that they contact the social worker to express their interest in caring for your children and get independent advice as soon as possible because decisions regarding looked-after children can be made quite rapidly.

Unrelated foster care

If there is no one in the family network who Children's Services think is suitable to care for your children, they must arrange for them to be cared for with unrelated foster-carers you don't know personally (or in some cases they could go into residential care).

If your children are in foster care with someone you don't know, it is a good idea to discuss with your social worker whether you can have contact with them. You may wish to thank them for looking after your children and let them know about your children's likes, dislikes and routines. Try to put this information across as "help". You don't want the foster-carer to think you are laying down the law about how to bring up your children. If you discuss the situation with them and ask how best you can support their care of your children, you will probably be able to establish a good working relationship. It is important to remember, though, that you will need to discuss this with your social worker first as to how much information you can share and how you can best communicate.

Working with your children's carer

Handing over your children to someone else can be very hard to accept. You may be grateful to the carer for taking on the care of your children. However, there are bound to be times when your idea of discipline or bedtimes or your values and views are very different to theirs. If your children's routine is disrupted just when their mum goes away, this can add to their confusion. So here are some tips that might be useful:

- As soon as possible after arriving in prison, write down (for the carer) your children's normal day, including out-of-school activities, bedtime routines, which books they like having read to them, favourite clothes, preferred food and normal ground rules. This can be the basis for discussion between you and the carer to ensure your children's lives stay as familiar as possible under the circumstances.

- It is important to accept that the carer may not be able to keep your children's routine exactly as it was; the children may have had to move house and school, for example. But if the carer is aware of these issues, it will make it easier for them and they will be less likely to mistakenly confuse or upset your children.

- Your children having a positive relationship with the carer is a sign that they are as happy as they can be, given the circumstances. If you are concerned about this, remind yourself that no one can ever replace you as your children's mum. Remember that all children have other special people in their lives and this is a good thing; they need a circle of people they can trust. Try to view the carer as a member of your children's caring circle.

- When small children haven't seen someone, even a parent, for a while, they might feel shy because that parent is very important to them and they may be scared of behaving in a way that the parent won't like. Try to be endlessly patient and understanding, even though this is far from easy. You will lose patience sometimes – you are only human. Try to patch things up sooner rather than later by apologising and explaining why you feel stressed.

- Remember to ask the carer how they are feeling – be a sympathetic ear for them, too. The relationship you have with your children's carer will affect your bond with your children. Of course, your first concern is for

your children, but their happiness also depends on the welfare of their carer. Grandparents are usually the ones who step in when a mother is away, but what they were able to do when you were small yourself may be a real effort for them now. Your sister may have taken on the role of carer for your children, even though she might already have kids of her own. Taking on your children will make life more challenging for her and she may feel some resentment – something you have done has now caused her life to become much busier and she may be experiencing unwanted pressures. For example, she may have your angry children shouting "You're not my mum!" at her when she asks them to stick to boundaries.

What matters most is your children's happiness and wellbeing. It is important that they do not feel they have to choose between you and their carer. You may have to bite your tongue if you see your children being well cared for, even if things are not being done in the same way that you would do them.

Adoption plans

In some cases, particularly when there are very young children or babies involved, Children's Services may consider placing children with people who may then go on to adopt them. It is essential that you get specialist legal advice from a solicitor as soon as possible in all cases, but especially if there is any mention of a plan for the adoption for your child. You can ask the prison staff to help you find a specialist solicitor.

Keeping in touch with your children

It is usually very important for your children (as well as for you) to be able to keep in touch with you while you are in prison – as long as this won't put your child at risk of harm. Whoever is caring for your children and whatever the legal arrangements, you should discuss with the carer or social worker what plans can be made for your children to visit, phone you regularly and write to you. The children's views will be important, too. If you have not managed to agree these things before going to prison, you can ask the prison staff to help you make necessary arrangements.

If there are things you don't like about how the carer is raising your children in your absence (for example, if they have introduced rules that you think aren't necessary, or you think they are letting your children get away with inappropriate behaviour), it is important to avoid using the children's visit to see you as a time to challenge their carer. Either telephone the carer later to discuss the issue or write them a letter setting out your concerns, stressing the fact that you want to support them overall, but that you have difficulty with some of their rules. Ask the prison staff to help you, if necessary.

Making a complaint

If you feel Children's Services have made the wrong decision about your children, or your views are not being taken into account, you can make a complaint. You can write to the Team Manager setting out your views and asking them to put things right or you can make a formal complaint in writing. Ask the social worker or the Team Manager to give you information about Children's Services complaints procedure. If you are not satisfied with their response you can then decide to complain to the Local Government Ombudsman.

Getting your children back

If your children are being looked after by a relative or friend under a private arrangement, or under a Section 20 agreement, you or any other person with parental responsibility can withdraw your agreement and ask for your children to be returned to your care. However, if the person caring for your children or Children's Services do not agree, they may well ask the court for an order to stop your children being removed or to keep your children where they are.

If your children are under a court order and you want them back, but this has not been agreed with the carer or Children's Services, you will need to apply to court for the order to be changed. However, you cannot ask for the court to reverse an adoption order. It is very important to get specialist advice about how best to get your children back. Whatever the situation, it is always a good idea to take advice from a specialist children's law solicitor before taking any steps to get your children back if you sense this is not agreed by their carer or social worker.

Some commonly used terms

If this is your first time in prison then you will probably be confused by all the terms that are used, so here is some guidance on what they mean. You need to discuss the terms with your social worker or a professional representative from Children's Services to make sure that you understand the terms used when they are applied to your case. You may also be able to get free advice from a solicitor under the legal aid scheme – ask the prison staff to help you arrange to discuss this with a specialist solicitor.

Accommodation This is when children are looked after in the care system with the agreement of the parent or another person who has parental responsibility. The parents retain parental responsibility and the local authority does not have it, although it is responsible for making plans that will promote the accommodated children's welfare.

In theory, it is possible for a person with parental responsibility to remove children from accommodation by simply informing Children's Services that this is what they want to do, but if Children's Services are not happy about this they can, and are very likely to, apply to court for an order to stop the children being removed. So it is always very important to get specialist legal advice before deciding to remove children from accommodation, especially if they have been there for some time.

Adoption If children are adopted, it means that all legal ties with their birth family are cut and the children are no longer legally part of that family. The children will have new birth certificates and a life-story book will be completed for their future. Adoption is final and the order cannot be reversed. Once adopted, the adoptive parents have parental responsibility for the children and make all decisions. The birth parents no longer have any parental responsibility or legal rights regarding the children. Financial support may be available to adoptive parents from adoption-support services following an assessment.

There is sometimes occasional contact (letters and photographs and very occasionally face-to-face contact) with the birth parents and relatives and the court has to consider what contact there should be when considering making an Adoption Order. If there is any mention of your children being placed for adoption, it is essential that you get legal advice immediately.

Care Order A Care Order (CO) is a court order that says that children will be looked after in the care system until they are 18 (unless the court discharges the order before then), even if the parents don't agree. It gives the local authority parental responsibility and, although they should consult the parents about plans for the children, they are able to override the parents' wishes if they think this is in the children's best interests.

The local authority must follow the duties regarding placement as for any looked-after children (see Looked-After Child on page 90).

It is possible that the court could make a Care Order or an Interim Care Order with the children at home, although the local authority would not normally apply to the court for this. The local authority has a duty to promote reasonable contact with the parents when a Care Order is made. Interim Care Orders are made during court proceedings and final orders made at the end of the proceedings.

Child Arrangements Order (formerly Residence and Contact Order – S.8 Children Act 1989) This is a new private law order, which can decide two things:

- **Where and with whom a children** will live (formerly known as a Residence Order). If a Child Arrangements Order (CAO) says that children should live with someone who is not their other parent, that person will have parental responsibility. This means that that person can make most decisions about the children (for example, agreeing to medical treatment) without having to get permission from others with parental responsibility. However, they cannot make some important decisions such as taking the children abroad for more than a month or changing their name or religion without the agreement of everyone with parental responsibility. If there is no agreement, the court will need to decide. There may be financial support available from the local authority, such as a Child Arrangements Order Allowance (CAOA) following an assessment of the children's/carer's needs, but this is discretionary.
- **Who children should see or be in touch with** (this used to be known as a Contact Order).

The order normally lasts until the child is 18 years old unless the court order says something different, but an application can be made to the court to end it sooner.

Contact Order This is an order that can be made in Care or Emergency Protection Order proceedings saying who your children should see or be in touch with. If there are no such proceedings, but a similar order is made it is called a Child Arrangements Order (see above).

An Emergency Protection Order An Emergency Protection Order (EPO) lasts for eight days and can be extended once for a further seven days. It can be discharged by the court sooner, otherwise it expires at the end of the period.

The local authority has parental responsibility and the parents have parental responsibility, although social services can override the parents' wishes if they think this is best for your children. This means that they can decide where the children should be placed and make the day-to-day decisions including concerning contact with the parents. They have a duty to consult with parents, but ultimately they will make the decisions they think are in the best interests of the children.

Family and Friends Care This is sometimes referred to as Kinship Care. This is when children are being looked after by a friend or another member of the family (usually grandparents or perhaps a sister) or when they are looked after by Children's Services and they are placed with a suitable family member or friend who has been approved as a foster-carer. Even if the care is provided by your family, there are still different legal statuses including:

- Your family may be assessed and approved by the local authority as foster carers **or**
- They may apply for a Child Arrangements Order for the

children to live with them **or**
- They may apply for a Special Guardianship Order **or**
- It may be a private arrangement between you and your family.

Foster for Adoption This is when the local authority places children for whom they are considering adoption with approved adopters on a temporary foster-care basis. This means that the foster-carers may go on to adopt the children after they have fostered them for some time. If this is suggested for your child it is essential that you take legal advice immediately.

Guardianship This is when a person is appointed by a parent with parental responsibility (or another guardian or a special guardian) to raise a child after their death. A guardian has parental responsibility for the child and this may be alongside anyone else who has parental responsibility for the child. They are entitled to a guardian's allowance.

Local authority foster-carer This is someone who has been assessed and approved by social services as being suitable to care for a Looked-After Child. A relative or friend can be approved as a foster-carer. All foster-carers have a right to receive a fostering allowance.

Looked-After Child This term (LAC) is used when a child under 18 is being looked after by Children's Services either in accommodation when parents/others with parental responsibility have agreed to this arrangement or because the court has made a CO or EPO.

The local authority is under a duty to first consider placing looked-after children with their other parent, subject to them being assessed, but if this arrangement is not suitable, then they should place them with other relatives who are assessed by the social worker as being suitable and have been approved as foster-carers. If neither option is suitable, then they must place the children with unrelated foster-carers or in residential care. Sometimes, where there is a plan for adoption, they may consider Foster for Adoption or applying for a placement order.

Parental Responsibility Parental Responsibility (PR) means the legal rights and responsibilities a parent has towards their children. As their mother, you will always have parental responsibility for them, but their father also has parental responsibility if:

- He is, or was, married to you, **or**
- His name is on your children's birth certificates as being the father after 1.12.2003, **or**
- If you agreed to him having parental responsibility in a formal agreement **or**
- If the court has made a Parental Responsibility Order.

Others who have parental responsibility include:
- The local authority, which obtains an Interim Care Order

or a Care Order;
- Anyone who is not a parent and who has a Child Arrangements Order saying the children will live with them or a Special Guardianship Order;
- A second female parent in some circumstances.

In some cases, another person with parental responsibility may make a decision you don't agree with, for example when Children's Services has a Care Order or there is a Special Guardianship Order. If you are not happy with a decision that someone else makes about your children, you can get advice about steps to take to challenge that decision.

Placement Order Children can only be placed for adoption (not the same as Foster for Adoption) if the parents with parental responsibility agree or the court has made a Placement Order, giving the local authority permission to place children with prospective adopters. This normally happens within or following a Care Order being made if the plan is for adoption. There are particular rules about applying to end this order, but you cannot apply to end it if your children are already placed with adopters.

Private arrangement This is when you have made an arrangement with a relative or friend to care for your children and there is no court order. You and anyone else with parental responsibility continue to have the right and authority to make decisions about your children, and the carer does not have that right. When you first make the arrangement with them it is a good idea to agree what they can decide about your children and to put this in writing.

Private fostering If your children are being raised by someone who is not a local authority-approved foster-carer or their grandparent, aunt, uncle, sibling or step-parent for a period of 28 days or more, this is known as a "private fostering arrangement". Both you and the person caring for the children must notify Children's Services of the arrangement and they have a duty to visit and monitor to check that the arrangements for your children are suitable. This includes visiting your children and their carer every six weeks to check that all is going well. Even where the private fostering arrangement is excellent, these visits have to take place, so it's important that you try to reassure the carer that this is not because Children's Services think that they are not doing a good job. It is just a legal requirement.

Supervision Order This is an order requiring the local authority to monitor the care of children. The local authority does not have parental responsibility, but it will "advise, assist and befriend the child" and the family. This type of order is usually applied for by the local authority when the children remain at home, but there are concerns about the parents' care which need to be monitored.

Residence Order This was an order which said where and with whom a child should live. It has now been replaced by a Child Arrangements Order (see page 89).

Special Guardianship Order A Special Guardianship Order (SGO) is a long-term order saying that children will live with the carer named in the order until they are 18 years of age. The order is very unlikely to be discharged before then, although it is possible if the court agrees to hear the application. This will only happen if there has been a significant change of circumstances since the order was made.

A SGO gives the carer parental responsibility and they have the right to override the parents' wishes. This means they can make all decisions regarding the care of the children except vitally important ones such as change of name or religion, adoption or adoption placements. If they want to take the children abroad for more than three months, they would need the agreement of everyone else who possesses parental responsibility or the permission of the court, but they can take the children abroad for under three months without discussing with anyone else who has parental responsibility.

If the parent does not agree with something the SGO has decided about the children's care they can apply to court to challenge them on a particular issue.

The local authority can give financial support and practical support under the Special Guardianship support services depending on an assessment of the needs of the children, special guardian or parent.

Summary

- People's experiences of the care system vary widely, but ultimately it is important to work with Children's Services (not against them). If you feel a decision is wrong, you should challenge it through the appeal process.
- It is not as common as you might fear that Children's Services take children into care and they can only do this if the court makes the necessary orders.
- Social workers do not expect mothers to be perfect; they just want them to be good enough for the children's welfare.
- Children's Services is able to give practical help to carers such as accessing furniture they need and getting children into a nearby school.
- The term Looked-After Child (LAC) refers to any child under 18 who is accommodated by the local authority (under S.20) or who is under a Care Order or Emergency Protection Order.
- Kinship Care is the term used when a child is being cared for by a family member or a friend, under a range of different legal arrangements.

Glossary of useful terms

Prisons and Children's Services are notorious for using shortened terms for systems or organisations. This guide will help you to make sense of some of the terms used which you may not be familiar with.

Prison terms

ACR Automatic Conditional Release

ACCT Assessment, Care in Custody & Teamwork

APF Action for Prisoners' Families

App Application – the form a prisoner fills out with a request

APVS Assisted Prison Visits Scheme

ARD Automatic Release Date

Association Prisoners' free time out of cell

B&B Bed & Breakfast

BASS Bail Accommodation & Support Service

BOSS Body Orifice Security Scanner (chair)

CAB Citizens Advice Bureau

CALM Controlling Anger & Learning to Manage it programme

CARATs Counselling Assessment Referral Advice & Through care services

CAT D Category D – Open (prison)

CDVP Community Domestic Violence Programme

CJA03 Criminal Justice Act 2003

CJA91 Criminal Justice Act 1991

CM Custody Manager

CRD Conditional Release Date

CRL Childcare Resettlement Licence

CSV Community Service Volunteer

DOM Director of Offender Management

DTO Detention & Training Order (for younger prisoners)

ECHR European Court of Human Rights

ETE Employment, Training & Education

FEW Family Engagement Worker

FNP Foreign National Prisoners

FOSAR Female Offender Specified Activity Requirement Order

HDC Home Detention Curfew (tagging)

HDCED Home Detention Curfew Eligibility Date

HMIP/HMCIP Her Majesty's Inspectorate of Prisons/ HM Chief Inspector of Prisons

HQ Headquarters

IDTS Integrated Drug Treatment Service

IEP Incentives & Earned Privileges

IMB Independent Monitoring Board

IND Immigration & Nationality Directorate

Induction Information given to new prisoners

IRS Incident Reporting System

ISP/IPP Indeterminate Sentence Prisoner/ Indeterminate Public Protection

KPT Key Performance Targets

MAPPA Multi-Agency Public Protection Arrangements

    MAPPA 1 – Overseen by 1 agency

    MAPPA 2 – Overseen by 2 agencies

    MAPPA 3 – Overseen by 3 agencies (high risk)

    MAPPA X – Number to be decided 6 months prior to release

MDT Mandatory Drug Testing

MHA Mental Health Act

MODCU Management of Detained Cases Unit

MOJ Ministry of Justice

MPQL Measuring Prisoners' Quality of Life

NFA No Fixed Abode

NOMS National Offender Management Service

OASys Offender Assessment System

OMU Offender Management Unit

Pad Cell

Pact Prison Advice and Care Trust

PECS Prisoner Escort & Custody Services

PED Parole Eligibility Date

PMU Population Management Unit

PPO Prolific & Priority Offender

PSO Prison Service Order (guidelines for prison staff)

Res Wing

RDR Resettlement Day Release

REO Race Equality Officer

ROR Resettlement Overnight Release

ROTL Release on Temporary Licence

SIR Security Information Report

SLA Service Level Agreement

SLED Sentence & Licence Expiry Date

SO Senior Officer

SPL Special Purpose Licence

SPVA Service Personnel & Veterans Agency

UAL Unlawfully at Large

VDT Voluntary Drug Testing

ViSOR Violent Sex Offenders Register

VO Visiting Order

VPU Vulnerable Prisoners Unit

YOI Young Offender Institution

Social services terms

CAF Child Assessment Framework
CAO Child Arrangements Order
CB Child Benefit
Child's Plan Plan drawn up for child deemed to be at risk
CHP Children's Hearing Panel
CO Care Order
CPCC Child Protection Case Conference
CPO Child Protection Order
CTB Council Tax Benefit
CTC Child Tax Credit
DWP Department for Work & Pensions
DLA Disability Living Allowance
EPO Emergency Protection Order
ESA Employment & Support Allowance
FGC Family Group Conferencing
GA Guardian's Allowance
HB Housing Benefit
HMRC Her Majesty's Revenue & Customs
IS Income Support
IBJSA Income Based JSA
JSA Job Seeker's Allowance
KC Kinship Carer
KFC Kinship Foster Carer
LA Local Authority
LAC Looked-After and accommodation Child
PC Pension Credit
PFC Private Foster Carer
PO Permanence Orders
PVG Protection of Vulnerable Groups scheme
PR Parental Responsibility
RO Residence Order
Safeguarder Person appointed to do report on child for hearing
SF Social Fund
SGO Special Guardianship Order
UC Universal Credit
WTC Working Tax Credit

Useful contacts

Women's Aid Federation of England, PO Box 391, Bristol BS99 7WS
T 0117 944 44 11 (general enquiries)
E info@womensaid.org.uk
W www.womensaid.org.uk; www.thehideout.org.uk
Freephone 24 Hour National Domestic Violence Helpline: 0808 2000 247 (run in partnership between Women's Aid and Refuge)
Wales Domestic Abuse Helpline: 0808 80 10 800 A free 24-hour, bilingual, gender-neutral and confidential helpline providing support and information to anyone experiencing domestic abuse, and to individuals and organisations seeking information or advice.
Broken Rainbow A service for lesbian, gay, bisexual and transsexual people who are experiencing domestic violence. Helpline: 0800 999 5428 (limited opening hours). **W** www.brokenrainbow.org.uk
Respond Support for Disabled Survivors
T 0808 808 0700 (limited opening hours).
Forced Marriage Helpline
T 0800 5999 247 (9 am–9 pm, 7 days a week).
Open Project run by Women's Rape & Sexual Abuse Centre (WRSAC) to support the needs of women offenders from Devon and Cornwall –
PO Box 39, Bodmin PL31 1XF
T 01208 77099 (Rape & Sexual Abuse Helpline)
T 01208 79992 (Domestic Violence Support Network)

FORWARD Support and advice about female genital mutilation. **T** 0208 960 4000
Women in Prison supports and campaigns for women offenders and ex-offenders, and assists women with advice on housing, education, mental health, legal rights, work, benefits, debt and domestic/sexual violence. **W** www.womeninprison.org.uk/ **T** Freephone advice line for offenders and ex-offenders: 0800 953 0125
Rights of Women offers women free legal rights advice on domestic and sexual violence, divorce, parenting and related issues. **T** 0207 251 6577/0207 490 2562 (textphone)
NSPCC offers advice for adults who are worried about a child. **T** 0808 800 5000 (24 hours).

Handbooks and guides
The Survivor's Handbook www.womensaid.org.uk/survivors-handbook
Breaking through: Women surviving male violence (Bristol: Women's Aid Federation of England, 1989). Includes personal stories, poems and cartoons, and ends with a section on "What we can do for ourselves" which gives positive suggestions that might help you.

Helplines

Remember that contact details can change, so if you can't get through check with your Family Engagement Worker for the updated contact details.

Name	Role	Telephone
Al-Anon	Support for someone worried about someone else's alcohol use.	0207 403 0888
Childline	Free 24-hour helpline for children	0800 1111
Families Anonymous (Famanon)	Support for families and friends concerned about a loved one's drug use	0845 1200 660
Family Rights Group	Providing family rights and kinship care support Advice line – Mon to Fri, 9.30 am–3 pm Kinship Carers' Group	0808 801 0366 0207 923 2628
Family Lives Parentline Plus	Free helpline for parents and carers, 7 am–midnight	0808 800 2222
Gingerbread/Lone Parent	Free helpline providing support and advice for single parents	0808 802 0925
Grandparents' Association	Advice and information for grandparents (office) Helpline – Mon to Fri, 10 am–4 pm	01279 428 040 0845 4349 585
Nacoa	National Association for the Children of Alcoholics	0800 358 3456
National Drugs Helpline (FRANK)	Free 24-hour helpline for anyone with concerns or questions about drugs.	0300 123 6600
NSPCC Child Protection	Free 24-hour helpline for those worried about the safety of a child	0808 800 5000
Offenders' Families Helpline	Free helpline for the families of offenders going through the criminal justice system	0808 808 2003
Post-Adoption Centre (PAC)	Support for birth relatives after a child has been adopted. Line open Mon, Tues, Fri, 10 am–4 pm. Wed 1 pm & 5 pm–7 pm, Thurs 2 pm–7 pm.	0207 284 5879
Prisoners' Families and Friends Service	Provides confidential one-to-one information and emotional support for prisoners' families, including a specialist service for families of sex offenders.	0808 808 3444
Release	Drugs helpline that also provides free legal advice on drug issues Mon to Fri 11 am–1 pm, 2 pm–4 pm	0207 324 2989
StepChange	Free helpline offering free debt advice Mon to Fri 8 am–8 pm, Sat 8 am–4 pm	0800 138 1111
YoungMinds	Free helpline offering advice, support and guidance to anyone concerned about the mental or emotional welfare of a young person up to 25 years of age. Mon to Fri 9.30 am–4 pm	0808 802 5544